KNIT SUPERHEROES!

KNIT SUPERHEROES!

REBECCA DANGER

12 ANIMALS—
CAPED, MASKED &
READY FOR
ACTION

Martingale®
Create with Confidence

Knit Superheroes!
12 Animals—Caped, Masked & Ready for Action
© 2016 by Rebecca Danger

Martingale®
19021 120th Ave. NE, Ste. 102
Bothell, WA 98011-9511 USA
ShopMartingale.com

Printed in China
21 20 19 18 17 16   8 7 6 5 4 3 2 1

**Library of Congress Cataloging-in-Publication Data
is available upon request.**

ISBN: 978-1-60468-612-8

MISSION STATEMENT

We empower makers who use fabric and yarn
to make life more enjoyable.

CREDITS

**PUBLISHER AND
CHIEF VISIONARY OFFICER**
Jennifer Erbe Keltner

CONTENT DIRECTOR
Karen Costello Soltys

MANAGING EDITOR
Tina Cook

ACQUISITIONS EDITOR
Karen M. Burns

TECHNICAL EDITOR
Ursula Reikes

COPY EDITOR
Marcy Heffernan

PRODUCTION MANAGER
Regina Girard

**COVER AND
INTERIOR DESIGNER**
Adrienne Smitke

PHOTOGRAPHER
Brent Kane

DEDICATION

To Maverick, my little superhero
and the inspiration for this book

18

24

30

42

48

55

66

72

78

CONTENTS

36

61

84

INTRODUCTION

HELLO AND WELCOME, FELLOW SUPERHERO ENTHUSIAST! This book combines two of my favorite things in the whole world: knitting and superheroes. I really, honestly don't know if it gets better than superheroes and knitting. Maybe if you throw in a cup of tea.

Though the mainstream action-packed superheroes have their charms, and are certainly entertaining, I have always loved the obscure underdog superheroes with the more unusual, and oftentimes not-so-helpful, superpowers. I have assembled an entire crew here for you to knit for your kids, your friends, or even yourself. As I knit through all the characters in this book, I grew very fond of each one, as well as the whole group. And I like to call them "An Extraordinary League of Knitted Superheroes," since they are just that.

So grab your favorite yarn and needles, a cup of tea (or beverage of choice), and get ready to use your superpowers to make some new friends.

Wishing you many happy knitting adventures,

Rebecca

SUPER SKILLS

In this section, you'll find specific information needed to knit the patterns in this book. Since you are a superhero knitter, I am assuming you know the majority of the terms and techniques in the patterns, and if you don't, you know you can use those super fingers to Google things you need help with, or go to my website. See "Even Superheroes Get Stuck" on page 17 for where to get help.

SUPER SKILL LEVEL

We know you've got superpowers—you can knit! I didn't include a skill-level rating on each pattern in this book since they are all rated Intermediate, for the knitter with some experience.

SUPER SAMPLES

I used two different yarns to make two samples for each superhero in this book.

* CoBaSi from Skacel (55% cotton, 21% elastic nylon, 16% bamboo, 8% silk; 50 g; 220 yds) **1**
  For this yarn I used a US 0 (2.0 mm) needle.

* Merino Worsted from Another Crafty Girl (100% superwash merino; 100 g; 215 yds) **4**
  For this yarn I used a US 4 (3.5 mm) needle.

Although I really, really love both of these yarns, don't feel like you have to buy a full skein of yarn for these projects! Most of the patterns really need less than 100 yards of any given color yarn, making this a great book to use up leftover yarn scraps. I listed how many yards of yarn I used for each color so you can check your stash before buying something new.

I used a sock weight and a worsted weight so you could get a general idea of how big your superheroes will turn out depending on what yarn and needle combination you use. Which brings us to the next section . . . gauge!

SUPER GAUGE

I don't list a specific gauge for any of the projects in this book. All of the patterns are written row by row (rather than "knit for 3"," or something like that) so that you can pick whatever size yarn and needles you want to use. Simply use smaller needles than those recommended for your yarn to create a tighter knit fabric so that the stuffing won't show through. My rule of thumb is to go down two or three needle sizes from those recommended for your yarn. As you can see, I used a US 4 (3.5 mm) needle on the Merino worsted, which is recommended to be knit on US size 5 to 7 needles. Depending on your personal knitting style and the yarn you are using, this may be right on for you, or you may want to try a different size. The best way to figure out what needles to use is to just start knitting. If it hurts your hands, your needle is too small. If you can easily see through your stitches, your needles are too big. Play around and figure out what works for you.

Because you can pick your yarn and needle size, you can make all sorts of sizes of superheroes from each one of the patterns. Just remember: bigger yarn and needles mean bigger superheroes, smaller yarn and needles mean smaller superheroes. Got it? Good. Let's get started!

SUPER TOOLS—NEEDLES

I knit all of these patterns using the magic loop method for working in the round because that is how I roll. I am a magic loop advocate. Pretty much you can't talk to me for more than 28.3 seconds without me asking if you use magic loop. (And that is what I actually call it, but my tech and copy editors always correct me and tell me it is "magic loop method" not "magic loop." They say if I am getting actual "magic" in my "magic loop," I am not sharing something with the rest of them. But I'm feeling like with my superheroes book, maybe that magic is my superpower.)

With the magic loop method, you use one circular needle with a long cable. But the magic loop method is just one way of working in the round. You can use double-pointed needles (dpns) or the magic loop method. If you have some other fancy-pants (or magical) way of working small-circumference projects in the round, you can use that. Use whatever is your preferred method of working small things in the round. You can use both the magic loop method and dpns too, in one project, if you want. I won't judge. Just go with the flow and do what works for you. Embrace those superpowers.

If you choose *not* to use the magic loop method and you run into a pattern that says something like, "Knit to last st on needle tip, K1f&b," this simply means to work to the center of your piece. So, as you get going, place a stitch marker between the two center stitches in your round, and when you see the above instructions, read it like this: "Knit to last st before marker, K1f&b." Kerpow! You've got this superhero knitting thing down like a pro.

WHAT TO KEEP IN YOUR UTILITY BELT

Since all of the patterns in this book need the same basic tool kit, I have included it here to avoid repetition in the patterns. You'll need:

* Scissors
* Tapestry needle
* Row counter (optional)
* Stuffing
* Straight pins for finishing

If anything else is needed that's not on this list, it will be included in the materials list for the pattern.

ABOUT THE CONSTRUCTION OF THE SUPERHEROES

Since I like to do as little finishing work as possible with my knitting so I have more time for hero work, I wrote all of the patterns in this book to be knit in one piece, eliminating as much finishing as I could. For the majority of non-removable parts (superheroes don't sleep in their capes!) you will place markers as you go, and come back to them later to pick up stitches and continue knitting.

This can be tricky, especially getting the first couple rounds going, so if you are uncomfortable with the whole picking-up-stitches thing, no worries! Instead of picking up, just cast on however many stitches the pattern calls for and knit the stitches from round 1. Easy, right? This can be done for all of the limbs in this book. Once you have all of your appendages and body finished, you'll need to whipstitch the limbs to the body.

TWO-AT-A-TIME LEGS

OK, I am excited about this one. For some of the superheroes, the legs and body are all knit as one piece. The following instructions will show you how easy this is to do. But for more detailed instructions, see my video tutorial at ShopMartingale.com/HowtoKnit. First of all, I do this using the magic loop method. If you want to use double-pointed needles, put your stitches on four needles and work the stitches with the fifth needle. Okey-dokey, here we go.

You'll be working both legs at the same time, so you'll need to work either from two balls of yarn, or from the inside and the outside of a center-pull ball. The legs begin with six (or whatever number the pattern indicates) stitches, so start by casting on half that number (three stitches in our example) with the first end of the yarn. Note that the following instructions are written for six stitches. These are the first three stitches of leg 1 (fig. 1).

Then using your other piece of yarn, cast on all six stitches of leg 2 (fig 2).

Divide your stitches to your two needle tips to set yourself up for working in the round. Using the magic loop method, slide your stitches down the cable of your needle and pull the cable out through the middle of your six stitches for leg 2 (fig 3).

(FIG. 1)

(FIG. 2)

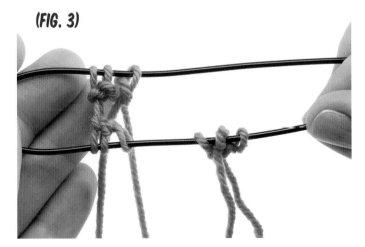

(FIG. 3)

(FIG. 4)

At this point, your front needle will have six stitches (three leg 1 stitches and three leg 2 stitches) and your back needle will have just three stitches from leg 2 (fig. 4).

Grab your working yarn from leg 1 and use the backward-loop cast on to cast on three more stitches for leg 1 onto your back needle. You'll have 12 stitches total, six on each needle (fig. 5), or the number required for your pattern.

There you go—two legs ready to work at the same time. Now, slide the stitches on the back needle onto the cable so you can use the needle tip to join for working in the round. You'll be joining the last stitch cast on (for leg 1) with the first stitch cast on (also for leg 1) (fig. 6).

To work two legs at the same time, work the first half of the stitches from leg 1 (fig. 7).

(FIG. 5)

(FIG. 6)

(FIG. 7)

KNIT SUPERHEROES!

Then drop that working yarn and pick up the working yarn attached to leg 2 (it will be hanging from the back set of stitches) (fig. 8).

Work the first half of the stitches of leg 2 on your front needle. When you run out of stitches on that needle, rotate around to your back needle with the same yarn (fig. 9).

Once you have worked through all the leg 2 stitches on your back needle, drop your working yarn from leg 2, pick up the working yarn for leg 1, and work the rest of the leg 1 stitches. This will complete one round (fig. 10).

Continue working both legs like this until you have worked the number of rounds called for in your pattern. Once you get to the last round, work the first half of the leg 1 stitches (fig. 11).

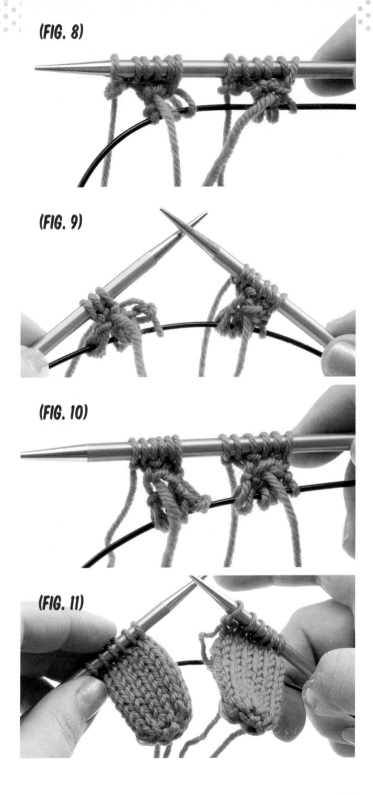

(FIG. 8)

(FIG. 9)

(FIG. 10)

(FIG. 11)

(FIG. 12)

(FIG. 13)

(FIG. 14)

(FIG. 15)

Turn your work so you are looking at the purl side of the fabric. Continuing with leg 1 working yarn, use the knitted cast on to cast on the six stitches between the legs (fig. 12).

Turn your work back to the right side, and using the yarn from leg 1, knit across all stitches of leg 2 (fig. 13).

Turn your work once again so that the wrong side is facing you. Using the yarn from leg 1, use the knitted cast on to cast on six stitches (fig. 14).

Turn your work once again and, continuing with the yarn from leg 1, knit the final six stitches of leg 1 (fig. 15). You should now have 36 stitches.

Place marker in first leg to mark the beginning of the round. At this point you can cut the yarn from leg 2. You'll continue knitting the body from this point. And you'll stuff and add safety eyes later through the hole you just created here with the additional cast-on stitches. Cool way of knitting the legs, right? I like it too.

KNIT SUPERHEROES!

SAFETY EYES

I like to use safety eyes, and occasionally a safety nose, since they are quick and easy to apply. However, you must think of your superhero's future owner before deciding to use safety eyes and noses. Children under three years of age should never be given toys with safety eyes or noses that could possibly come off and be ingested. It's just as easy to embroider eyes and noses as it is to use safety eyes and noses, and they won't pose a choking hazard.

EVEN SUPERHEROES GET STUCK

I know you'd rather have these pages filled with patterns than a bunch of directions for things you likely already know how to do (you're a superhero knitter, after all). So, if a term or technique has got you confused, hop onto a superhero's best friend: the Internet! I recorded video tutorials for techniques used in my book *50 Yards of Fun*, and you can find them at ShopMartingale.com/HowtoKnit. You'll find:

* How to work a Turkish (invisible) cast on
* How to knit stuffed rings and Kitchener stitch (including how to work provisional cast on using waste yarn)
* How to knit I-cord on two double-pointed needles
* Knitting in the round: magic loop method
* How to pick up knitting stitches for arms, legs, and more
* How to add fringe to knitted toys

Alternatively, when you buy your supplies at a local yarn shop the staff will (generally) be more than happy to help with any knitting questions you might have. Local yarn shops often have classes that may help as well. You could even ask them if they would do a class using this book!

Alrighty, that's it for the boring parts. Now on to the patterns. Go! Get knitting!

RANDOLPH RACCOON

• REPUTABLE REFRESHMENT RESPONDER •

Flying, leaping large buildings, X-ray vision, super strength; these are all normal superhero abilities. **RANDOLPH, HOWEVER, IS NOT YOUR TYPICAL SUPERHERO.** His superpower? Making chocolate bars appear. It doesn't always help him fight crime, but he certainly makes friends easily!

SAMPLES

COBASI SOCK YARN (below)

* Approx 11" from head to toe
* Colors: Seattle Sky 038, Black 002, Natural 003, Vavava Voom Red 054
* 9 mm black safety eyes
* 15 mm black triangular safety nose

MERINO WORSTED (at right)

* Approx 17" from head to toe
* Colors: Foil (gray), Casting Shadows (black), Natural, Pomegranate
* 15 mm black safety eyes
* 21 mm black triangular safety nose

MATERIALS

YARN

Gray: 70–110 yds for raccoon

Black: 45–70 yds for mask, paws, feet, and tail

White: 40–60 yds for pants, snout, and tail

Red: 100–160 yds for pants and cape

NEEDLES

36" or longer circular needle 2 or 3 sizes smaller than those recommended for your yarn (for magic loop method) for body and cape

2 double-pointed needles in same size as circular needle for I-cord

NOTIONS

Basic supplies (see "What to Keep in Your Utility Belt" on page 12)

15 removable st markers (or 14 removable st markers and 1 fixed marker)

2 safety eyes (see "Samples" for sizes)

1 triangular safety nose (see "Samples" for sizes)

LEGS

Using black and referring to "Two-at-a-Time Legs" (page 13), CO 6 sts per leg.

Rnd 1: (K1f&b, K1, K1f&b) twice. (10 sts each leg)

Rnd 2: K1f&b in all sts. (20 sts each leg)

Rnds 3–12: Knit all sts.

Rnds 13–36: With gray, knit all sts.

Rnds 37–47: Starting with red, knit all sts in stripe patt of 3 rnds red, 3 rnds white.

Rnd 48: Cont in white, K10 sts of first leg, use knitted CO to CO 5 sts, cont with yarn from leg 1 for rest of rnd, knit across all 20 sts of leg 2, use knitted CO to CO 5 sts, knit final 10 sts of rnd. Cut yarn from leg 2. You'll be stuffing and adding safety eyes later through hole created here. (50 sts)

BODY

Rnds 1–19: Starting with red, knit all sts in est stripe patt of 3 rnds red, 3 rnds white. After rnd 19, place removable markers in sts 35 and 41 to mark for tail.

Rnds 20–22: Cont in red, knit all sts.

Rnds 23–56: With gray, knit all sts. Place removable markers as you work:

> **Rnd 48:** PM in sts 3, 22, 28, and 47 to mark for arms.

> **Rnd 53:** PM in sts 9 and 17 to mark for snout.

At end of rnd 56 switch to black to work next 9 rnds.

Rnd 57: (Ssk, knit to end of needle tip) twice. (48 sts)

Rnd 58: Knit all sts.

Rnd 59: (Knit to last 2 sts on needle tip, K2tog) twice. (46 sts)

Rnd 60: Knit all sts. Place removable markers in sts 8 and 16 to mark for snout.

Rnds 61–72: Rep rnds 57–60. Do not PM. On rnd 66, switch to gray and cont in gray to top of head. (34 sts). Place removable markers as you work:

> **Rnd 70:** PM in sts 2, 17, 20, and 34 to mark for ears.

Rnds 73–75: Rep rnds 57–59. (30 sts)

Rnd 76: (K1, ssk, knit to last 3 sts on needle tip, K2tog, K1) twice. (26 sts)

Rnd 77: Rep rnd 76. (22 sts)

Turn body inside out and use 3-needle BO to BO all sts. Turn RS out.

SNOUT

Rnd 1: Using circular needle and starting at marked st 9 on rnd 53, pick up 9 sts, 1 per st to marked st 17 by slipping needle under existing sts to put loops on needle. (You will not be knitting sts until rnd 2.) Then, move over 1 st, and up 1 st from last st picked up, and pick up 1 st per rnd for 6 rnds. (15 sts). Slide sts onto cable to set up for magic loop method and heading in opposite direction, start at marked st 16 on rnd 60, pick up 9 sts, 1 per st to marked st 8. Finally, move down 1 st and over 1 st from last picked-up st and pick up 1 st per rnd for 6 rnds. (30 sts). Move last 3 picked-up sts onto first needle tip and last 3 sts from first needle onto second needle tip to set beg of rnd in center side of nose. PM to indicate beg of rnd. Using white, work all subsequent rnds using magic loop method.

Rnds 2–7: Knit all sts.

Rnd 8: (Ssk, knit to end of needle tip) twice. (28 sts)

Rnd 9: (Knit to last 2 sts on needle tip, K2tog) twice. (26 sts)

Rnds 10 and 11: Rep rnds 8 and 9. (22 sts)

FACE

TAIL

Rnd 12: (K1, ssk, knit to 3 sts on needle tip, K2tog, K1) twice. (18 sts)

Rnd 13: Rep rnd 12. (14 sts)

Rnd 14: K2tog around. (7 sts)

Stuff nose. Cut yarn and use a tapestry needle to pull through rem sts, but only close nose halfway. Place backing of triangle nose on 1 ridge or 2, leaving a space between backer and nose. Pop nose into open end of snout, then pull snout closed around nose. Secure by sewing and looping around nose a couple times as you weave in ends.

ARMS

Rnd 1: Using gray and starting at marked st 47 on rnd 48, PU 7 sts, 1 per st to marked st 3. Slide sts to cable to set up for magic loop method and heading in opposite direction, PU same 7 sts 1 rnd up.

(14 sts). PM in first picked-up st of rnd to indicate beg of rnd.

Rnds 2–36: Knit all sts.

Rnds 37–47: With black, knit all sts.

Rnd 48: K2tog around. (7 sts)

Stuff arm. Cut yarn and using a tapestry needle, pull tail through rem sts to close.

Rep with marked sts 22 and 28 on rnd 48 for other arm.

EARS

Rnd 1: Using gray and starting at marked st 2 on rnd 70, PU 10 sts, 1 per st up toward top of head. First 7 or 8 sts will be from dec rnds of head, and final 2 or 3 sts will be on 3-needle BO seam. Slide sts to cable to set up for magic loop method, and heading in opposite direction, PU same 10 sts down back of head toward marked

st 34 on rnd 70. (20 sts). PM in first picked-up st of rnd to indicate beg of rnd.

Rnds 2–5: Knit all sts.

Rnd 6: (Ssk, K8) twice. (18 sts)

Rnd 7: Knit all sts.

Rnd 8: (K7, K2tog) twice. (16 sts)

Rnd 9: Knit all sts.

Rnd 10: (K1, ssk, K2, K2tog, K1) twice. (12 sts)

Rnd 11: (K1, ssk, K2tog, K1) twice. (8 sts)

Rnd 12: (Ssk, K2tog) twice. (4 sts)

Stuff ear if desired (samples' ears are unstuffed). Cut yarn and using a tapestry needle, pull tail through rem sts to close.

Rep with marked sts 17 and 20 on rnd 70 for other ear.

WHEREVER THERE IS DANGER, I'LL BE THERE WITH CHOCOLATE!

TAIL

Rnd 1: Using black and starting at marked st 35 on rnd 19, PU 7 sts, 1 per st to marked st 41. Slide sts to cable to set up for magic loop method and heading in opposite direction, PU same 7 sts 1 row up. (14 sts). PM in first picked-up st of rnd to indicate beg of rnd.

Rnds 2–4: Knit all sts.

Beg working in stripe patt of 4 rnds white, 4 rnds black as follows.

Rnd 5: With white, (K1f&b, knit to last st on needle tip, K1f&b) twice. (18 sts)

Rnd 6: Knit all sts.

Rnds 7–12: Rep rnds 5 and 6. (30 sts)

Rnd 13: (K7, K1f&b, K7) twice. (32 sts)

Rnds 14–56: Knit all sts.

Rnd 57: (K1, ssk, knit to last 3 sts on needle tip, K2tog, K1) twice. (28 sts)

Rnd 58: Knit all sts.

Rnds 59–66: Rep rnds 57 and 58. (12 sts)

Rnd 67: K2tog around. (6 sts)

Stuff tail. Cut yarn and using a tapestry needle, pull tail through rem sts to close.

CAPE AND TIES

CAPE

Cape is knit flat (back and forth), not in the round.

Using red, CO 25 sts. Do not join.

Rows 1 and 2: (K1, P1) across to last st, K1.

Row 3: K1f&b, (P1, K1) across to end of row. (26 sts)

Row 4: K1f&b, (P1, K1) across to last st, P1. (27 sts)

Rows 5 and 6: (P1, K1) across to last st, P1.

Row 7: K1f&b, (K1, P1) across to end of row. (28 sts)

Row 8: K1f&b, (K1, P1) across to last st, K1. (29 sts)

Rows 9–56: Rep rows 1–8 another 6 times. (53 sts)

Rows 57–100: Rep rows 1 and 2 another 22 times.

Loosely BO all sts in patt.

TIES

Ties are knit as an I-cord (see page 92).

Using red and a dpn, PU 3 sts from one side of narrower end of cape. Work these sts as an I-cord for 50 rnds, or until I-cord is long enough to tie in a bow around neck. Cut yarn and using a tapestry needle, pull tail through rem sts to close.

Rep above direction on opposite side of narrower end of cape to create second tie.

FINISHING RANDOLPH

Weave in any rem ends. Stuff body and add safety eyes. If you want, embroider a belly button using black yarn, securing ends inside of body. Finally, whipstitch opening between legs shut. Ta-dah! Finished Super Racoon. Now tie on his cape and go make some chocolate appear!

SUPERSIZE

Want to supersize your superhero? For more caped, masked, and action fun, knit your superhero with 3 strands of worsted-weight yarn held together on size 13 (9 mm) needles. Use black safety eyes, 24 mm or larger, and the largest triangle nose you can find.

CRUNCH! MUNCH!

RANDOLPH RACCOON

LUCKY LANCELOT
• LEGENDARY LION •

BEING A LION IS PRETTY MUCH ALL THE SUPERPOWER THAT ONE REALLY NEEDS.

Lucky Lancelot takes full advantage of this fact, slaps on his wristbands, lucky belt, and knee-high boots, and roams the streets to make this world a safer place. Unfortunately, being a lion, he generally scares most folks out of whatever they are doing. Since he rarely sees anyone doing anything they shouldn't be, he feels he is very successful in his safety endeavors.

SAMPLES

COBASI SOCK YARN (below)

* Approx 19" from head to toe
* Colors: Gold Crest 057, Carrot 070, Kiwi 007, Turkish Coffee 035
* 9 mm black safety eyes
* 12 mm black oval safety eye for nose

MERINO WORSTED (at right)

* Approx 27" from head to toe
* Colors: Citrus, Tangerine, Good Fortune, Chocolate/Caramel
* 15 mm black safety eyes
* 24 mm black oval safety eye for nose

MATERIALS

YARN

Gold: 200–275 yds for lion

Orange: 90–120 yds for eye mask, boots, and belt

Green: 30–50 yds for wristbands and belt buckle

Brown: 30–50 yds for mane and end of tail

NEEDLES

36" or longer circular needle in a size 2 or 3 sizes smaller than those recommended for your yarn (for magic loop method)

Spare needle, any style, in same size as circular needle (for 3-needle BO)

NOTIONS

Basic supplies (see "What to Keep in Your Utility Belt" on page 12)

17 removable st markers (or 16 removable st markers and 1 fixed marker)

2 safety eyes (see "Samples" for sizes)

1 oval or round safety eye for nose (see "Samples" for sizes)

24

BODY

Lancelot begins at base of body.

Using gold yarn and Turkish CO (page 93), wrap 24 loops (for 48 sts) onto circular needle. PM to indicate beg of rnd and beg body using magic loop method.

Rnd 1: Knit all sts from Turkish CO to beg working in the round. Place removable markers in sts 1, 7, 18, and 24 to mark for legs.

Rnd 2: (K1f&b, knit to last st on needle tip, K1f&b) twice. (52 sts)

Rnds 3–10: Rep rnds 1 and 2. Do not PM. (68 sts)

Rnds 11–60: Knit all sts. Place removable markers as you work:

> **Rnd 22:** PM in sts 15 and 20 to mark for tail.

Rnd 61: (Ssk, knit to last st on needle tip, K2tog) twice. (64 sts)

Rnds 62 and 63: Knit all sts.

Rnds 64–78: Rep rnds 61–63. (44 sts)

Rnd 79: (Ssk, K18, K2tog) twice. (40 sts). Place removable markers in sts 4, 17, 24, and 37 to mark for arms.

Rnds 80 and 81: Knit all sts.

Rnd 82: Rep rnd 61. (36 sts)

Rnds 83–85: Knit all sts.

Rnd 86: (K2tog, K1) around. (24 sts)

Rnds 87–89: Knit all sts.

Rnd 90: [K1f&b twice, (K1f&b, K1) 4 times, K1f&b twice] twice. (40 sts)

Rnd 91: Knit all sts.

Rnd 92: [(K1f&b, K1) twice, (K1f&b, K2) 4 times, (K1f&b, K1) twice] twice. (56 sts)

Rnds 93–109: Knit all sts. Place removable markers as you work:

> **Rnd 97:** PM in sts 37 and 48 to mark for nose.

> **Rnd 106:** PM in sts 37 and 48 to mark for nose.

Rnds 110–117: With orange, knit all sts.

Rnds 118–120: With gold, knit all sts. Cont working in gold to top of head. At end of rnd 120, place removable marker in sts 1 and 29 to mark for ears.

Rnd 121: Knit all sts.

Rnd 122: (K2tog, K5) around. (48 sts)

Rnd 123: Knit all sts.

Rnd 124: (K2tog, K2) around. (36 sts)

Rnd 125: Knit all sts.

Stuff body and add safety eyes.

Rnd 126: (K2tog, K1) around. (24 sts)

Rnd 127: K2tog around. (12 sts)

Finish stuffing. Cut yarn and using a tapestry needle, pull tail through rem sts to close.

NOSE

Rnd 1: Using circular needle, start at marked st 37 on rnd 97, pick up 12 sts, 1 per st to marked st 48 by slipping needle under existing sts to put loops on needle. (You will not be knitting sts until rnd 2.) Then move over 1 st, and up 1 st from last st picked up, and pick up 1 st per rnd for 8 rnds. (20 sts). Slide sts onto cable to set up for magic loop method and heading in opposite direction, start at marked st 48 on rnd 106, pick up 12 sts, 1 per st to marked st 37. Finally, move down 1 st and over 1 st from last picked-up st and pick up 1 st per rnd for 8 rnds. (40 sts). Move last 4 sts on needle onto first needle tip and last 4 sts on first needle onto second needle tip. This will arrange sts so beg of rnd is on side of nose. PM to indicate beg of rnd. Using gold, go back and work this rnd and all subsequent rnds using magic loop method.

Rnds 2–6: Knit all sts.

Rnd 7: (K3, K2tog) around. (32 sts)

Rnd 8: Knit all sts.

Rnd 9: K2tog around. (16 sts)

Rnd 10: Knit all sts.

Rnd 11: K2tog around. (8 sts)

Stuff nose. Cut yarn and use a tapestry needle to pull through rem sts, but only close nose halfway. Pop the nose and backing on 1 ridge or 2,

FACE

BELT

leaving a space between backer and nose. Pop nose into open end of snout, then pull yarn to close snout around nose. Secure by sewing and looping around nose a couple times as you weave in ends.

ARMS

Rnd 1: Using gold and starting in marked st 37 on rnd 79, PU 8 sts to marked st 4, 1 st per rnd. Slide sts to cable to set up for magic loop method and heading in opposite direction, PU same 8 sts 1 rnd up. (16 sts). PM in first picked-up st of rnd to indicate beg of rnd.

Rnds 2–65: Knit all sts. After rnd 65, place removable marker in sts 1 and 9 to mark for wristbands.

Rnd 66: [K1f&b twice, (K1, K1f&b) twice, K1f&b twice] twice. (28 sts)

Rnds 67–86: Knit all sts.

Rnd 87: K2tog around. (14 sts)

Stuff hand. Cut yarn and using a tapestry needle, pull tail through rem sts to close arm.

Rep with marked sts 17 and 24 on rnd 79 to make other arm.

LEGS

Rnd 1: Using gold and starting in marked st 7 on rnd 1, PU 10 sts to marked st 1, PU 1 st per rnd, for a total of 7 sts from base of body, and 3 sts from inc bumps up side. Slide sts to cable to set up for magic loop method, move toward front of body 1 st and heading in opposite direction, PU same 10 sts. (20 sts). Be sure beg of rnd is toward back of body so that heel will be in correct spot. PM in first picked up st of rnd to indicate beg of rnd.

Rnds 2–44: With gold, knit all sts.

Rnds 45–80: With orange, knit all sts. You'll rem in orange to end of boot.

Work heel back and forth on first 10 sts of rnd and holding last 10 sts of rnd on your cable.

Row 1: Sl 1, knit to end. Turn.

Row 2: Sl 1, purl to end. Turn.

Rows 3–10: Rep rows 1 and 2 another 4 times.

WORK BOOT

Rnd 1: Knit across 10 heel sts again, using same needle tip, PU 6 sts from gusset edge. Slide sts to cable to set up for magic loop method and use empty needle tip to knit 10 held sts, using same needle tip, PU 6 sts from gusset edge. (32 sts). PM in next st to be knitted to indicate new beg of rnd.

Rnd 2: K10, (K2tog) twice, K14 to last 4 sts, (ssk) twice. (28 sts)

Rnd 3: Knit all sts.

Rnd 4: K10, (K2tog) twice, K10 to last 4 sts, (ssk) twice. (24 sts)

Rnds 5–30: Knit all sts.

Rnd 31: K2tog around. (12 sts)

Stuff foot. Cut yarn and using a tapestry needle, pull tail through rem sts to close.

Rep from rnd 1 of leg with marked sts 18 and 24 on rnd 1 to make other leg.

EARS

Rnd 1: Using gold and starting in marked st 1 on rnd 120, PU 7 sts, 1 st per rnd toward top of head. Slide sts to cable to set up for magic loop method and heading in opposite direction, PU same 7 sts down back of head. (14 sts). PM in first picked-up st of rnd to indicate beg of rnd.

Rnd 2: (K3, K1f&b, K3) twice. (16 sts)

Rnds 3–8: Knit all sts.

Rnd 9: K2tog around. (8 sts)

Stuff ear if desired (samples' ears are unstuffed). Cut yarn and using a tapestry needle, pull tail through rem sts to close ear.

Rep with marked st 29 on rnd 120 (moving to front of body instead of back) to make other ear.

TAIL

Rnd 1: Using gold and starting in marked st 15 on rnd 22, PU 6 sts, 1 per st to marked st 20. Slide sts to cable to set up for magic loop method and heading in opposite direction, PU same 6 sts 1 row up. (12 sts). PM in first picked-up st of rnd to indicate beg of rnd.

Rnds 2–75: Knit all sts.

Cut yarn and using a tapestry needle, pull tail through rem sts to close. Cut 12 pieces of brown, 6" long, for fringe. Holding 4 pieces tog for each fringe, attach fringe in 3 spots along end of tail. Trim even to about ¾".

MANE

The mane is knit back and forth in rows, not in the round.

Using brown and circular needle, CO 84 sts. DO NOT JOIN.

Rows 1–6: Knit all sts (garter st).

Begin points.

Row 1: K12. Turn.

Row 2: Ssk, knit to end. Turn. (11 sts)

Rows 3–11: Rep row 2. (2 sts at end of row 11)

Cut yarn and using a tapestry needle, pull tail through rem sts to finish point.

Move on to next 12 sts, join yarn and rep rows 1–11 until all sts have been worked. (7 points)

WRISTBANDS

Rnd 1: Using green and starting in marked st 1 on rnd 65 of arm, PU 8 sts, 1 per st to marked st 9. Slide sts to cable to set up for magic loop method and heading in opposite direction, PU same 8 sts on opposite side of arm. (16 sts). Check that as you knit, cuff will head up arm (not over hand). PM in first picked-up st of rnd to indicate beg of rnd.

Rnds 2 and 3: Knit all sts.

Rnd 4: (K1f&b, knit to end of needle tip) twice. (18 sts)

Rnds 5 and 6: Knit all sts.

Rnd 7: (Knit to last st on needle tip, K1f&b) twice. (20 sts)

Rnds 8 and 9: Knit all sts.

Rnds 10–21: Rep rnds 4–9. (28 sts)

Rnd 22: (K1, P1) around.

Loosely BO in patt.

Rep with markers on other arm to make other wristband.

BELT AND BELT BUCKLE

You can adjust length of belt to fit your lion; just measure as you go and stop when it fits. Both belt and buckle are knit flat (back and forth), not in the round.

BELT

With orange, use provisional CO to CO 8 sts. DO NOT JOIN.

Rows 1–150: Knit all sts (garter st).

Place provisional CO sts onto empty needle tip and use 3-needle BO to finish ends.

BELT BUCKLE

Using green, CO 8 sts. DO NOT JOIN.

Row 1: Purl all sts.

Row 2: K1f&b, knit to last 2 sts, K1f&b, K1. (10 sts)

Row 3: Purl all sts.

Rows 4–9: Rep rows 2 and 3 another 3 times. (16 sts)

Rows 10–15: Work all rows in St st.

Row 16: Ssk, knit to last 2 sts, K2tog. (14 sts)

Row 17: Purl all sts.

Rows 18–23: Rep rows 16 and 17 another 3 times. (8 sts)

Loosely BO all sts.

"L" FOR BELT BUCKLE

The L is knit flat (back and forth), not in the round.

Using orange, CO 8 sts. DO NOT JOIN.

Rows 1 and 2: Knit all sts (garter st).

Row 3: BO first 5 sts, knit rem sts.

Rows 4–18: Knit all sts.

Loosely BO all sts.

FINISH LANCELOT

Weave in ends. Pin mane around head and using tapestry needle and yarn to match mane, use a running st or whipstitch to sew in place. Block "L" and belt buckle as desired. Pin "L" to belt buckle and using tapestry needle and yarn to match "L," sew in place using a running st. Place belt buckle on seam in belt, and using tapestry needle and yarn to match buckle, sew in place over seam using a running st. Put belt on Lancelot, and go fight some crime.

FEAR NOT, CITIZENS! I AM HERE TO SUBDUE ALL OUTLAWS!

THE MAGNIFICENT MOO

• MARVELOUS, MASTERFUL MESMERIST •

Moo is a Belted Galloway cow, which is why she has a white stripe around her middle. From a young age she noticed that folks stare at her black-and-white midsection, and by accident a few times, she managed to put her onlookers into a near trance by moving slightly. Realizing this, SHE WENT TO HYPNOTIST SCHOOL AND LEARNED HOW TO HYPNOTIZE PEOPLE AND USE THE ART OF SUGGESTION to get people to do what she wants. Now she has taken up hero work and uses her power to help fight crime.

SAMPLES

COBASI SOCK YARN (below)

* Approx 9" from nose to tail; 11" from head to toe
* Colors: Black 002, Natural 003, Gun Metal Grey 037, Bubblegum 021, Vavava Voom Red 054, Royal (029)
* 9 mm black safety eyes
* ½"-diameter button

MERINO WORSTED (at right)

* Approx 12" from nose to tail; 16" from head to toe
* Colors: Licorice (black), Natural, Foil (gray), Bubblegum, Hibiscus, Blueberry
* 15 mm black safety eyes
* 1⅛"-diameter button

MATERIALS

YARN

Black: 170–210 yds for cow

White: 50–80 yds for cow

Gray: 30–50 yds for hooves

Pink: 20–30 yds for udder

Red: 80–100 yds for mask and cape

Blue: 60–80 yds for cape

NEEDLES

36" or longer circular needle in a size 2 or 3 sizes smaller than those recommended for your yarn (for magic loop method)

NOTIONS

Basic supplies (see "What to Keep in Your Utility Belt" on page 12)

13 removable st markers (or 12 removable st markers and 1 fixed marker)

2 safety eyes (see "Samples" for sizes)

1 button to close Moo's cape (size depends on finished cow size)

Sewing needle and thread to attach button

30

BODY

Moo begins at back end of body.

Using black and Turkish CO (page 93), wrap 30 loops (for 60 sts) onto circular needle. PM to indicate beg of rnd and beg body using magic loop method.

Rnd 1: Knit all sts from Turkish CO to beg working in the round.

Rnd 2: (K1f&b, knit to last st on needle tip, K1f&b) twice. (64 sts) Place removable markers in sts 32 and 36 to mark for tail.

Rnds 3–6: Rep rnds 1 and 2. Do not PM. (72 sts)

Rnds 7–25: With black, knit all sts. Place removable markers as you work:

Rnd 7: PM in sts 5 and 68 to mark for legs.

Rnd 13: PM in st 72 to mark for udder.

Rnd 16: PM in sts 6 and 67 to mark for legs.

Rnds 26–50: With white, knit all sts. Place removable markers as you work:

Rnd 30: PM in st 1 to mark for udder.

Rnds 51–70: With black, knit all sts. You'll rem in black to front of body. Place removable markers as you work:

Rnd 60: PM in sts 5 and 68 to mark for legs.

Rnd 69: PM in sts 6 and 67 to mark for legs.

Rnd 71: (Ssk, knit to last 2 sts on needle tip, K2tog) twice. (68 sts)

Rnd 72: Knit all sts.

Rnds 73 and 74: Rep rnds 71 and 72. (64 sts)

Rnd 75: Rep rnd 71. PM in sts 15 and 31 to mark placement for sewing on head. (60 sts)

Stuff body. Cut yarn, leaving a generous tail and work Kitchener st to close.

TAIL

Rnd 1: Using black and starting in marked st 30 on rnd 2, PU 5 sts, 1 st per rnd toward marked st 36. Slide sts to cable to set up for magic loop method and heading in opposite direction, PU same 5 sts 1 rnd over. (10 sts) PM in first picked-up st of rnd to indicate beg of rnd.

Rnds 2–45: With black, knit all sts.

Rnds 46–59: With gray, knit all sts.

Rnd 60: (Ssk, K1, K2tog) twice. (6 sts)

Stuff tail lightly. Cut yarn, leaving a generous tail and work Kitchener st to close.

UDDER

Rnd 1: Using pink and starting in marked st 72 on rnd 13, PU 18 sts, 1 st per rnd away from tail. Slide sts to cable to set up for magic loop method and starting with marked st 1 from rnd 30, heading in opposite direction, PU same 18 sts 1 st over. (36 sts). PM in first picked-up st of rnd to indicate beg of rnd.

Rnds 2–12: Knit all sts.

Rnd 13: (Ssk, knit to last 2 sts on needle tip, K2tog) twice. (32 sts)

Rnd 14: Rep rnd 13. (28 sts). Place removable marker in sts 2, 6, and 11 to mark for teats.

Stuff udder lightly. Cut yarn, leaving a generous tail and work Kitchener st to close.

ADD TEATS

Rnd 1: Using pink and starting in marked st 2 on rnd 14 of udder, PU 3 sts, 1 st per rnd. Slide sts to cable to set up for magic loop method and heading in opposite direction, PU same 3 sts 1 st over. (6 sts) PM in first picked-up st of rnd to indicate beg of rnd.

Rnds 2–5: Knit all sts.

Cut yarn and using a tapestry needle, pull tail through rem sts to close.

Rep rnds 1–5, starting in marked st 6, then in marked st 11 from rnd 14 to make 2 more teats. There will be 2 udder sts between each teat.

FACE

UDDER

LEGS

Rnd 1: Using black and starting in marked st 68 on rnd 7, PU 10 sts, 1 st per rnd away from tail. Slide sts to cable to set up for magic loop method and starting with marked st 67 from rnd 16, heading in opposite direction, PU same 10 sts 1 st over. (20 sts). PM in first picked-up st of rnd to indicate beg of rnd.

Rnds 2–40: With black, knit all sts.

Rnds 41–50: With gray, knit all sts.

Rnd 51: Cont with gray, K2tog around. (10 sts)

Stuff leg up to body. Cut yarn, leaving a generous tail and work Kitchener st to close.

Rep with other marked sts to knit Moo's other 3 legs.

HEAD

Using white and Turkish CO, wrap 14 loops (for 28 sts) onto circular needle. PM to indicate beg of rnd and beg head using magic loop method.

Rnd 1: Knit loops from Turkish CO to beg working in the round.

Rnd 2: (K1f&b, knit to last st on needle tip, K1f&b) twice. (32 sts)

Rnd 3: Knit all sts.

Rnds 4–7: Rep rnds 2 and 3. (40 sts)

Rnds 8–16: Knit all sts.

Rnd 17: (Ssk, knit to end of needle tip) twice. (38 sts)

Rnd 18: Knit all sts.

Rnd 19: (Knit to last 2 sts on needle tip, K2tog) twice. (36 sts)

Rnd 20: With black, knit all sts. Cont in black to top of head.

Rnds 21–28: Rep rnds 17–20. (28 sts)

Rnds 29 and 30: Knit all sts.

Rnd 31: (K1f&b, knit to end of needle tip) twice. (30 sts)

Rnd 32: Knit all sts.

Rnd 33: (Knit to last st on needle tip, K1f&b) twice. (32 sts)

Rnd 34: Knit all sts.

Rnds 35–38: Rep rnds 31–34. (36 sts)

Rnds 39–45: Knit all sts. After rnd 45, place removable marker in sts 18 and 36 to mark for ears.

Rnd 46: (Ssk, knit to last 2 sts on needle tip, K2tog) twice. (32 sts)

Rnd 47: Knit all sts.

Rnds 48–51: Rep rnds 46 and 47. (24 sts)

Rnd 52: Rep rnd 46. (20 sts)

Stuff head. Add eyes, and embroider nostrils. Cut yarn, leaving a generous tail and work Kitchener st to close.

EARS

Rnd 1: Using black and starting in marked st 36 on rnd 45, PU 6 sts, 1 st per rnd toward top of head. Slide sts to cable to set up for magic loop method and heading in opposite direction, PU same 6 sts 1 st over. (12 sts). PM in first picked-up st of rnd to indicate beg of rnd.

Rnds 2 and 3: Knit all sts.

Rnd 4: (K1f&b, knit to end of needle tip) twice. (14 sts)

Rnd 5: Knit all sts.

Rnd 6: (Knit to last st on needle tip, K1f&b) twice. (16 sts)

Rnd 7: Knit all sts.

Rnds 8–21: Rep rnds 4–7 another 3 times, then rep rnds 4 and 5 once more. (30 sts)

Rnd 22: K2tog around. (15 sts)

Rnd 23: K2tog around to last 3 sts, K3tog. (7 sts)

Stuff ear if desired (samples' ears are unstuffed). Cut yarn and using a tapestry needle, pull tail through the rem sts to close.

Rep with marked st 18 on rnd 45 to make other ear.

CAPE BAND AND CAPE

Both are knit flat (back and forth), not in the round.

BAND

Using red, CO 6 sts. DO NOT JOIN.

Rows 1–4: Knit all sts (garter st).

Row 5 (buttonhole): K2, BO 2 sts, knit to end. (4 sts)

Row 6 (buttonhole): K2, cable CO 2 sts, knit to end. (6 sts)

Rows 7–12: Knit all sts. Place removable marker in last st of row 12.

Rows 13–60: Knit all sts. Place removable marker in last st of row 60 (on same side as first marker).

Rows 61–72: Knit all sts.

Loosely BO all sts.

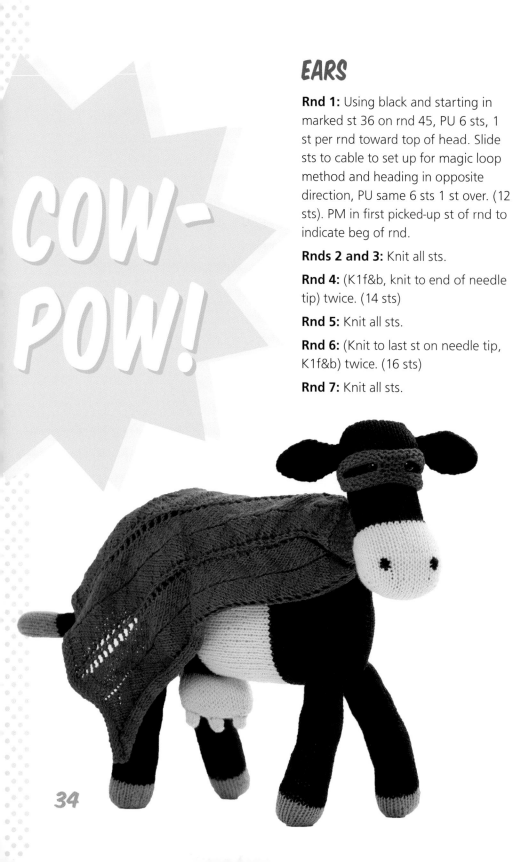

COW-POW!

CAPE

Row 1 (set-up row RS): Using blue and starting in marked st on row 12 of cape band, PU 26 sts, 1 st per garter ridge to the marked st on row 60. (26 sts). Cont to knit back and forth to finish cape.

Row 2: With blue, K1f&b 26 times. (52 sts)

Row 3: With blue, knit all sts.

Row 4: With blue, P1f&b, purl to last 2 sts, P1f&b, P1. (54 sts)

Row 5: With red, K5, (YO, K5, ssk, K2tog, K5, YO, K1) twice, YO, K5, ssk, K2tog, K5, YO, K5.

Row 6: With red, purl all sts.

Rows 7 and 8: With red, rep rows 5 and 6.

Rows 9–12: With blue, rep rows 5 and 6 twice.

Rows 13–84: Rep rows 5–12, keeping in est stripe patt of 4 rows red, 4 rows blue (21 total stripes including where it attaches to cape band).

Rows 85–88: With red, knit all rows (garter st).

Loosely BO all sts.

MASK

Mask is knit flat (back and forth), not in the round.

Using red, CO 60 sts. DO NOT JOIN.

Row 1: K2tog, knit to last st, K1f&b.

Row 2: K1f&b, knit to last 2 sts, K2tog.

Rows 3 and 4: Rep rows 1 and 2 once more.

Row 5: K2tog, K21, BO 6 sts, K3 (4 sts between BO sts), BO 6 sts, K19 to last st, K1f&b. (48 sts rem)

Row 6: K1f&b, K21, cable CO 6 sts, K4, cable CO 6 sts, K20 to last 2 sts, K2tog. (60 sts)

Rows 7–10: Rep rows 1 and 2 twice more.

Loosely BO all sts.

FINISH MOO

Weave in ends. Pin Moo's head to end opposite of her tail, using markers on rnd 75 for placement. Using a tapestry needle and black yarn, attach to body using a whipstitch. Pin button to non-buttonhole end of cape band so that it lines up with buttonhole. Sew in place using needle and thread. Put on Moo's cape and mask and find someone to hypnotize.

35

DIXON DACHSHUND

• DARING DOGGIE DO-RIGHT •

Dixon used to be very timid and reserved. One day, while walking down an alley to avoid some bullies, Dixon happened across a pair of red-and-yellow undies, complete with a hole for his tail. He picked them up, took them home, and washed them. When he pulled them out of the dryer and slipped them on, ALL OF A SUDDEN HE COULD FLY! IMAGINE HIS DELIGHT! Now he flies around looking for others who are being bullied to protect them, since folks tend not to tease a flying dog.

SAMPLES

COBASI SOCK YARN (below)

* Approx 14" from head to toe
* Colors: Turkish Coffee 035, Vavava Voom Red 054, Butter Cream 042
* 9 mm black safety eyes

MERINO WORSTED (at right)

* Approx 24" from head to toe
* Colors: Chocolate/Caramel, Pomegranate, Citrus
* 15 mm black safety eyes

MATERIALS

YARN

Brown: 275–350 yds for dachshund

Red: 80–100 yds for head and wristbands and undies

Yellow: 40–60 yds for undies

Scrap black yarn for nose

Waste yarn for holding live sts

NEEDLES

36" or longer circular needle in a size 2 or 3 sizes smaller than those recommended for your yarn (for magic loop method)

NOTIONS

Basic supplies (see "What to Keep in Your Utility Belt" on page 12)

17 removable st markers (or 16 removable st markers and 1 fixed marker)

2 safety eyes (see "Samples" for sizes)

BODY

Dixon begins at base of body.

Using brown and Turkish CO (page 93), wrap 14 loops (for 28 sts) onto circular needle. PM to indicate beg of rnd and beg body using magic loop method.

Rnd 1: Knit all sts from Turkish CO to beg working in the round. Place removable markers in sts 25 and 28 to mark for legs.

Rnd 2: (K1f&b, knit to last st on needle tip, K1f&b) twice. (32 sts)

Rnd 3: Knit all sts.

Rnds 4–13: Rep rnds 2 and 3. (52 sts)

Rnds 14–72: Knit all sts. Place removable markers as you work:

> **Rnd 25:** PM in sts 36 and 43 to mark for tail.

At end of rnd 72, beg to stuff body. Cross-stitch belly button with scrap black yarn (samples' are around rnd 30), tying ends inside of body.

Rnd 73: (K1, ssk, knit to last 3 sts on needle tip, K2tog, K1) twice. (48 sts)

Rnd 74: Knit all sts.

Rnds 75–78: Rep rnds 73 and 74 twice. (40 sts). After rnd 78, place removable markers in sts 4, 17, 24, and 37 to mark for arms.

Rnd 79: Rep rnd 73. (36 sts)

Rnds 80–82: Knit all sts.

Rnd 83: (K1f&b, K16, K1f&b) twice. (40 sts)

Rnds 84–115: Knit all sts. Place removable markers as you work:

> **Rnd 88:** PM in sts 5 and 16 to mark for nose.

> **Rnd 103:** PM in sts 5 and 16 to mark for nose.

Rnd 116: (K1, ssk, knit to last 3 sts on needle tip, K2tog, K1) twice. (36 sts)

Rnd 117: Knit all sts.

Rnds 118–121: Rep rnds 116 and 117 twice. (28 sts). After rnd 121, place removable markers in sts 4, 11, 18, and 25 to mark for ears and add more stuffing.

Rnds 122–124: Rep rnd 116. (16 sts)

Finish stuffing. Using markers on rnd 103 as a guide, add safety eyes. Cut yarn, leaving a generous tail and work Kitchener st to close.

NOSE

Rnd 1: Using circular needle and starting in marked st 5 on rnd 88, pick up 12 sts, 1 per st to marked st 16 by slipping needle under existing sts to put loops on needle. (You will not be knitting sts until rnd 2.) Then, move over 1 st, and up 1 st from last st picked up, and pick up 1 st per rnd for 14 rnds. (26 sts). Slide sts onto cable to set up for magic loop method and heading in opposite direction, start in marked st 16 on rnd 103, pick up 12 sts, 1 per st to marked st 5. Finally, move down 1 st and over 1 st from last picked up and pick up 1 st per rnd for 14 rnds. (52 sts). Move last 7 picked-up sts onto first needle tip and last 7 sts on first needle onto second needle tip to set beg of rnd in center side of nose. PM to indicate beg of rnd. Using brown, go back and work this rnd and all subsequent rnds using magic loop method.

Rnds 2–10: Knit all sts.

Rnd 11: (Ssk, knit to end of needle tip) twice. (50 sts)

Rnd 12: Knit all sts.

Rnd 13: (Knit to last 2 sts on needle tip, K2tog) twice. (48 sts)

Rnd 14: Knit all sts.

Rnds 15–22: Rep rnds 11–14. (40 sts)

Rnds 23–25: Rep rnds 11–13. (36 sts)

Rnd 26: With scrap black yarn, knit all sts. Cont with black to end of nose.

Rnd 27: (K2, K2tog) around. (27 sts)

Rnd 28: Knit all sts.

Beg to stuff nose.

Rnd 29: (K1, K2tog) around. (18 sts)

Rnd 30: Knit all sts.

Rnd 31: K2tog around. (9 sts)

Finish stuffing. Cut yarn and using a tapestry needle, pull tail through rem sts to close.

FACE

TAIL

ARMS

Rnd 1: Using brown and starting in marked st 37 on rnd 78, PU 8 sts to marked st 4, 1 st per rnd. Slide sts to cable to set up for magic loop method and heading in opposite direction, PU same 8 sts 1 rnd up. (16 sts). Be sure beg of rnd is toward back of body for correct paw shaping, PM.

Rnds 2–38: Knit all sts.

Rnd 39: K1f&b 8 times, K8. (24 sts)

Rnds 40–54: Knit all sts.

Rnd 55: K2tog around. (12 sts)

Rnd 56: Knit all sts.

Rnd 57: K2tog around. (6 sts)

Stuff hand. Cut yarn and using a tapestry needle, pull tail through rem sts to close arm.

Rep with marked sts 17 and 24 on rnd 78 to make other arm.

LEGS

Rnd 1: Using brown and starting in marked st 28 on rnd 1, work toward outside of body and PU 5 sts from base of body and 4 sts from incs up side for 9 total sts. Slide sts to cable to set up for magic loop method, move toward front of body 1 st, and heading in opposite direction, PU same 9 sts. (18 sts). Be sure beg of rnd is toward back of body so that heel will be in correct spot, PM.

Rnds 2–40: Knit all sts.

Work heel back and forth on first 9 sts of rnd and holding last 9 sts of rnd on cable.

Row 1: Sl 1, knit to end. Turn.

Row 2: Sl 1, purl to end. Turn.

Rows 3–8: Rep rows 1 and 2 another 3 times.

WORK FOOT

Rnd 1: Knit across 9 heel sts again. Using same needle tip, PU 5 sts from gusset edge. Slide sts to cable to set up for magic loop method and use empty needle tip to knit 9 held sts. Using same needle tip, PU 5 sts from gusset edge. (28 sts). PM in next st to be knitted to indicate new beg of rnd.

Rnd 2: Knit all sts.

Rnd 3: K9, (K2tog) twice, knit to last 4 sts, (ssk) twice. (24 sts)

Rnd 4: Knit all sts.

Rnd 5: K9, K2tog, knit to last 2 sts, ssk. (22 sts)

Rnds 6–22: Knit all sts.

Rnd 23: K2tog around. (11 sts)

Stuff foot. Cut yarn and using a tapestry needle, pull tail through rem sts to close foot.

Rep with marked st 25 on rnd 1 to make other leg.

EARS

Rnd 1: Using brown and starting in marked st 25 on rnd 121, PU 8 sts, 1 st per rnd toward the marker in st 4. Slide sts to cable to set up for magic loop method and heading in opposite direction PU same 8 sts 1 rnd up. (16 sts). PM in first picked-up st of rnd to indicate beg of rnd.

Rnd 2: (K1f&b, knit to end of needle tip) twice. (18 sts)

Rnd 3: Knit all sts.

Rnd 4: (Knit to last st on needle tip, K1f&b) twice. (20 sts)

Rnd 5: Knit all sts.

Rnds 6–29: Rep rnds 2–5. (44 sts)

Rnds 30–44: Knit all sts.

Rnd 45: (K1, ssk, knit to last 3 sts on needle tip, K2tog, K1) twice. (40 sts)

Rnd 46: Knit all sts.

Rnds 47–56: Rep rnds 45 and 46. (20 sts)

Rnd 57: Rep rnd 45. (16 sts)

Stuff ear if desired (samples' ears are unstuffed). Cut yarn and using a tapestry needle, pull tail through the rem sts to close ear.

Rep with marked sts 11 and 18 on rnd 121 to make other ear.

TAIL

Rnd 1: Using brown and starting with marked st 36 on rnd 25, PU 8 sts, 1 per st to marked st 43. Slide sts to cable to set up for magic loop method and heading in opposite direction, PU same 8 sts 1 rnd up. (16 sts). PM in first picked-up st of rnd to indicate beg of rnd.

Rnds 2–74: Knit all sts.

Rnd 75: K2tog around. (8 sts)

Cut yarn and using a tapestry needle, pull tail through rem sts to close.

WRISTBANDS

Make 2.

Using red and circular needle, CO 24 sts. PM to indicate beg of rnd and beg using magic loop method.

Rnds 1–8: (K2, P2) around.

Loosely BO in patt.

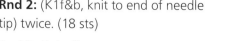

BOW-WOW!

ANKLEBANDS

Make 2.

Using red and circular needle, CO 28 sts. PM to indicate beg of rnd and beg band using magic loop method.

Rnds 1–10: (K2, P2) around.

Loosely BO in patt.

HEADBAND

Using red and circular needle, CO 44 sts. PM to indicate beg of rnd and beg band using magic loop method.

Rnds 1–5: (K2, P2) around.

Loosely BO in patt.

UNDIES

With yellow, use provisional CO to CO 30 sts. DO NOT JOIN.

Row 1: Knit all sts.

Row 2: Purl all sts.

Row 3: K1, ssk, knit to last 3 sts, K2tog, K1. (2 st dec)

Row 4: P1, P2tog, purl to last 3 sts, P2tog tbl, P1. (2 st dec)

Rows 5–11: Rep rows 3 and 4 another 3 times, then rep row 3 once more. (12 sts)

Rows 12–20: Starting with a purl row, work 9 rows in St st.

Row 21: K1, K1f&b, knit to last 3 sts, K1f&b, K2. (2-st inc)

Row 22: P1, P1f&b, purl to last 3 sts, P1f&b, P2. (2-st inc)

Rows 23–29: Rep rows 21 and 22 another 3 times, then rep row 21 once more. (30 sts)

Rows 30–32: Starting with a purl row, work 3 rows in St st.

Beg working in the round.

Rnd 1 (set-up rnd): Place sts from provisional CO onto back needle, knit across sts you've been working, beg to work in rnd using magic loop method and rotate to back needle tip to knit provisional CO sts. (60 sts)

Rnds 2–12: Knit all sts.

Rnd 13 (tail hole): K10, BO 10 sts, knit to end of rnd.

Rnd 14 (tail hole): K10, use knitted CO to CO 10 sts, knit to end of rnd.

Rnds 15–22: Knit all sts.

Rnd 23: With red, (K2, P2) around. You'll rem in red for rest of undies.

Rnds 24–27: (K2, P2) around.

Loosely BO all sts.

FINISH LEG OPENINGS

Rnd 1: Using red and circular needle, PU 36 sts around leg opening. (You can pick up more or fewer sts depending on your piece, just be sure it's a multiple of 4.)

Rnds 2 and 3: (K2, P2) around.

Loosely BO all sts in patt.

Rep to finish other leg opening.

MAKE "Y" ON UNDIES

Row 1: Find center rib in waistband on front of undies, PU 2 sts.

Rows 2–24: Knit all sts (garter st).

Row 25: K1f&b twice. (4 sts)

Row 26: Knit all sts.

Row 27: K2. Turn. Cont knitting just these 2 sts. Other 2 sts can rem on cable; you'll come back to them later.

Rows 28–44: Knit all sts.

Loosely BO sts.

Go back to 2 live sts and join in yarn. Finish "Y" by rep rows 27–44.

FINISH DIXON

Using a tapestry needle and matching yarn, st the "Y" to front of undies using a running st. Use photo on page 40 for reference for where ends should line up on leg openings. Weave in rem ends. Slip Dixon's bands on his wrists, ankles, and head, and slip him into his undies. Tah-dah! Done, dachshund, done. Now fly, dachshund, fly!

GLOBETROTTING GERALD

• GUARDIAN GIRAFFE •

A giraffe is sort of an awkward animal, with a fairly large body balanced on spindly legs and knobby knees, and with a ridiculously long neck. But, **GERALD WAS BLESSED WITH THE SUPERPOWER OF SUPER ELASTICITY.** He can stretch and bend and twist every body part, and manipulate himself into any shape he wants, making him perfect to be a master yogi. Gerald travels the world to share his yoga with others, fighting crime wherever he ends up.

SAMPLES

COBASI SOCK YARN (below)

* Approx 9" long; 22" from head to toe
* Colors: Gold Crest 057, Turkish Coffee 035, Seafoam 101, Natural 003
* 9 mm black safety eyes

MERINO WORSTED (at right)

* Approx 12" long; 29" from head to toe
* Colors: Saoirse (gold), Earth, Pool, Natural
* 15 mm black safety eyes

MATERIALS

YARN

Gold: 190–250 yds for giraffe

Brown: 50–75 yds for horns, hooves, spots, and tail fringe

Aqua: 90–110 yds for mask and cape

White: 60–90 yds for cape

NEEDLES

36" or longer circular needle in a size 2 or 3 sizes smaller than those recommended for your yarn (for magic loop method)

Spare circular needle in same size as main needle, any length (for holding live sts)

NOTIONS

Basic supplies (see "What to Keep in Your Utility Belt" on page 12)

13 removable st markers (or 12 removable st markers and 1 fixed marker)

2 safety eyes (see "Samples" for sizes)

LEGS

Make 4.

Using brown and main circular needle, CO 6 sts. PM to indicate beg of rnd and beg leg using magic loop method.

Stuff legs as you work.

Rnd 1: With brown, K1f&b 6 times. (12 sts)

Rnds 2–12: With brown, knit all sts.

Rnds 13–65: With gold, knit all sts.

Cut yarn, leaving a generous tail, and place sts on spare needle.

Rep rnds 1–65 another 2 times, placing leg sts onto spare needle so that half of sts are on front needle tip and half are on back needle tip (setting yourself up to knit in rnd using magic loop method). Knit 4th leg, leaving working yarn attached.

BODY

Rnd 1: Knit first 6 sts of 4th leg, cable CO 5 sts, knit first 6 sts of leg 3 from spare needle, cable CO 20 sts, knit first 6 sts of leg 2 from spare needle, cable CO 5 sts, knit first 6 sts of leg 1 from spare needle. Rotate needle tips so sts you have just worked are on cable and you are ready to knit second half of body sts onto back needle (magic loop method). Knit last 6 sts of leg 1 from spare needle, cable CO 5 sts, knit last 6 sts of leg 2 from spare needle, cable CO 20 sts, knit last 6 sts of leg 3 from spare needle, cable CO 5 sts, knit last 6 sts of leg 4 from spare needle. (108 sts). PM to mark beg of rnd and cont to work body using magic loop method.

Rnds 2–35: Knit all sts.

Rnd 36: K1, ssk, knit to last 3 sts, K2tog, K1. (106 sts)

Rnd 37: Knit all sts.

Rnds 38–43: Rep rnds 36 and 37. (100 sts). After rnd 43, place removable markers in sts 2 and 99 to mark for tail.

Rnd 44: Rep rnd 36. (98 sts)

Rnd 45: Working first 33 sts and last 33 sts of rnd, cut yarn leaving a generous tail and work Kitchener st to close back. (32 sts)

Beg neck. Neck is created from rem 32 sts.

Rnds 1–5: Knit all sts.

Rnd 6: K1, ssk, knit to last 3 sts, K2tog, K1. (30 sts)

Rnds 7–24: Rep rnds 1–6. (24 sts)

Rnds 25–75: Knit all sts.

Rnd 76: K12, hold 2 needle tips tog and with working yarn make 16 loops as for Turkish CO. Hold yarn to back to make sure last loop is secure, pull out back needle tip and cont to work in rnd to end of rnd. Only second half of new sts have been worked. Work first half in next rnd. (32 sts added, 56 total)

Rnd 77: Knit all sts.

Rnd 78: Knit to last st on front needle tip, K1f&b, K1f&b, knit to end. (58 sts)

Rnds 79–82: Rep rnds 77 and 78. (62 sts)

Rnds 83–92: Knit all sts.

Rnd 93: Knit to last 3 sts on front needle, K2tog, K1, K1, ssk, knit to end. (60 sts)

Rnd 94: Knit all sts.

Rnds 95 and 96: Rep rnd 93. (56 sts)

Rnd 97: K13, place next 30 sts on waste yarn. Bring yarn across gap and cont to work in rnd and knit to end of rnd. (26 sts on needles)

Rnds 98–102: Knit all sts.

Rnd 103: (Ssk, knit to last 2 sts on needle, K2tog) twice. (22 sts)

Rnd 104: Knit all sts. Place removable marker in sts 1 and 12 to mark for ears.

Rnds 105 and 106: Rep rnds 103 and 104. Do not PM. (18 sts)

Rnd 107: Rep rnd 103. (14 sts)

Stuff head and add the eyes now if you wish. (You'll still have access through tummy or nose once top of head is closed.) Cut yarn, leaving a generous tail and work Kitchener st to close head.

Place held nose sts on needles. Beg on nose side, attach yarn by tying it to nose, and work Kitchener st to close nose.

EARS

Rnd 1: Using gold and starting in marked st 1 on rnd 104, PU 4 sts, 1 st per rnd toward top of head. Slide sts to cable to set up for magic loop method and heading in opposite direction, move over 1 st and PU same 4 sts down back of head. (8 sts). PM in first picked-up st of rnd to indicate beg of rnd.

Rnds 2 and 3: Knit all sts.

Rnd 4: (K1f&b, K3) twice. (10 sts)

Rnd 5: Knit all sts.

Rnd 6: (K4, K1f&b) twice. (12 sts)

Rnd 7: Knit all sts.

Rnd 8: (K1f&b, K5) twice. (14 sts)

Rnds 9–14: Knit all sts.

Rnd 15: (Ssk, knit to last 2 sts on needle tip, K2tog) twice. (10 sts)

Rnd 16: Knit all sts.

Rnd 17: Rep rnd 15 (6 sts)

Stuff ear if desired (samples' ears are unstuffed). Cut yarn and using a tapestry needle, pull tail through rem sts to close.

Rep with marked st 12 on rnd 104 to make other ear.

TAIL

Rnd 1: Using gold and starting in marked st 99 on rnd 43, PU 4 sts, 1 st per st toward marked st 2. Slide sts to cable to set up for magic loop method and heading in opposite direction, PU same 4 sts up 1 rnd. (8 sts). PM in first picked-up st of rnd to indicate beg of rnd.

Rnds 2–44: Knit all sts.

Use 3-needle BO to close all sts. Cut 10 pieces from brown, 6" long, for fringe. Holding 2 pieces tog at a time, add fringe in center of end of tail. Then add 2 fringes to left and 2 fringes to right of center fringe. Trim all fringe even to about ¾".

HORNS

Placement is based on ear placement.

Rnd 1: Using brown and starting in st directly next to an ear, PU 3 sts, 1 st per st toward the other ear. Slide sts to cable to set up for magic loop method and heading in opposite direction, PU same 3 sts 1 st back. (6 sts). PM in first picked-up st of rnd to indicate beg of rnd.

Rnds 2–8: Knit all sts.

Rnd 9: K1f&b 6 times. (12 sts)

Rnds 10–15: Knit all sts.

Rnd 16: K2tog around. (6 sts)

Stuff if desired (samples' horns are unstuffed). Cut yarn and using a tapestry needle, pull tail through the rem sts to close.

Rep, starting on opposite side with st closest to other ear to make other horn.

GLOBETROTTING GERALD

SPOTS

FACE

SPOTS

All spots are knit in brown.

SMALL

Make 2.

Using circular needle, CO 4 sts. PM to indicate beg of rnd and beg spot using magic loop method.

Rnd 1: K1f&b 4 times. (8 sts)

Rnd 2: Knit all sts.

Rnd 3: K1f&b 8 times. (16 sts)

Rnd 4: Knit all sts.

Loosely BO all sts.

MEDIUM

Make 6.

Work as for Small through rnd 4.

Rnd 5: (K1f&b, K1) around. (24 sts)

Rnd 6: Knit all sts.

Loosely BO all sts.

LARGE

Make 2.

Work as for Medium through rnd 6.

Rnd 7: (K1f&b, K2) around. (32 sts)

Rnd 8: Knit all sts.

Loosely BO all sts.

CAPE BAND AND CAPE

Band is knit in the round and cape is knit flat (back and forth).

BAND

Using aqua and circular needle, CO 36 sts. PM to indicate beg of rnd and beg band using magic loop method.

Rnds 1–6: (K2, P2) around. After rnd 1, place removable marker on CO edge below sts 1 and 24 to mark for cape.

Loosely BO in patt.

CAPE

Row 1 (set up): Using white and starting in marked st 24, PU 24 sts, 1 st per garter ridge to marked st 1.

Row 2: Knit all sts (garter st).

Row 3: K2, YO, knit to last 2 sts, YO, K2. (26 sts)

Row 4: Knit all sts.

Row 5: With aqua, K2, YO, knit to last 2 sts, YO, K2. (2 st inc)

Rows 6–8: Knit all sts.

Rows 9–108: Rep rows 5–8 working in est stripe patt of 4 rows white, 4 rows aqua. (78 sts)

Row 109: With aqua, K2, YO, (K2tog, K1, YO) to last 4 sts, K2, YO, K2. (80 sts)

Rows 110–112: With aqua, knit all sts (garter st).

Loosely BO all sts.

KNIT SUPERHEROES!

MASK

Mask is knit flat (back and forth), not in the round.

Using aqua, CO 72 sts. DO NOT JOIN.

Row 1: K2tog, knit to last st, K1f&b.

Row 2: K1f&b, knit to last 2 sts, K2tog.

Rows 3 and 4: Rep rows 1 and 2 once more.

Row 5: K2tog, K26, BO 6 sts, K3 (4 sts between BO sts), BO 6 sts, knit to last st, K1f&b. (60 sts)

Row 6: K1f&b, K28, cable CO 6 sts, K4, cable CO 6 sts, knit to last 2 sts, K2tog. (72 sts)

Rows 7–10: Rep rows 1 and 2 twice more.

Loosely BO all sts.

FINISH GERALD

Stuff body and add safety eyes. Weave in ends on spots and arrange them on body as desired, pinning in place. With a tapestry needle and matching yarn, use a running st to sew spots in place. Weave in all rem ends. With a tapestry needle and matching yarn, use a whipstitch to close up Gerald's tummy. Slip on his cape, tie on his mask, and fight some super villains!

STAY WHERE YOU ARE, EVILDOERS! GERALD IS HERE WITH HIS FLEXIBLE LONG ARMS OF THE LAW!

ALBERTO ALLIGATOR

• AMAZING ELVIS IMPERSONATOR •

Alberto Alligator's superpower is a siren song that can distract even the nastiest of super villains. But it comes with a catch: his superpower works only with Elvis songs. The bright side is he can get anyone to do anything Elvis sings about. So, HE WON'T LET ANYONE STEP ON YOUR BLUE SUEDE SHOES, AND HE CAN GET SUPER VILLAINS ALL SHOOK UP. Unfortunately, he does have a lot of super villains in love with him, thanks to Elvis's plethora of love songs.

SAMPLES

COBASI SOCK YARN (below)

* Approx 16" from snout to tail
* Colors: Natural Olive 008, Black 002, Gold Crest 057
* 9 mm black safety eyes
* ¾"-diameter button

MERINO WORSTED (at right)

* Approx 24" from snout to tail
* Colors: Good Fortune (green), Licorice, Zest
* 15 mm black safety eyes
* 1⅛"-diameter button

MATERIALS

YARN

Green: 190–290 yds for alligator

Black: 110–150 yds for cape

Yellow: 30–50 yds for star on cape

NEEDLES

36" or longer circular needle in a size 2 or 3 sizes smaller than those recommended for your yarn (for magic loop method)

NOTIONS

Basic supplies (see "What to Keep in Your Utility Belt" on page 12)

11 removable st markers (or 8 removable st markers and 3 fixed markers)

2 safety eyes (see "Samples" for sizes)

1 button to close Alberto's cape (size depends on finished size)

Sewing needle and thread to attach button

48

BODY

Alberto begins at the nose.

Using green and Turkish CO (page 93), wrap 12 loops (for 24 sts) using circular needle. PM to indicate beg of rnd and beg body using magic loop method.

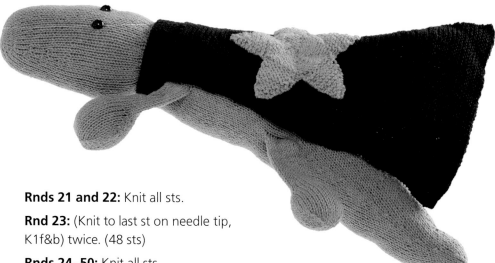

Rnd 1: Knit all sts from Turkish CO to beg working in the round.

Rnd 2: (K1f&b, knit to last st on needle tip, K1f&b) twice. (28 sts)

Rnd 3: Knit all sts.

Rnd 4: (K1f&b, knit to last st on needle tip, K1f&b) twice. (32 sts)

Rnd 5: Knit all sts.

Rnd 6: (K1f&b, knit to last st on needle tip, K1f&b) twice. (36 sts)

Rnd 7: Knit all sts.

Rnd 8: (K1f&b, knit to end of needle tip) twice. (38 sts)

Rnds 9 and 10: Knit all sts.

Rnd 11: (Knit to last st on needle tip, K1f&b) twice. (40 sts)

Rnds 12 and 13: Knit all sts.

Rnd 14: (K1f&b, knit to end of needle tip) twice. (42 sts)

Rnds 15 and 16: Knit all sts.

Rnd 17: (Knit to last st on needle tip, K1f&b) twice. (44 sts)

Rnds 18 and 19: Knit all sts.

Rnd 20: (K1f&b, knit to end of needle tip) twice. (46 sts)

Rnds 21 and 22: Knit all sts.

Rnd 23: (Knit to last st on needle tip, K1f&b) twice. (48 sts)

Rnds 24–50: Knit all sts.

Rnd 51: (K2tog, K1) around. (32 sts)

Rnds 52–54: Knit all sts.

Rnd 55: (K1f&b, K1) around. (48 sts)

Rnd 56: K6, PM, K5, K1f&b, K6, PM, knit to end of rnd. (49 sts)

Rnd 57: K1f&b, knit to marker, SM, K1, (P1, K1) 6 times, SM, knit to end of needle tip, K1f&b, knit to end of rnd. (51 sts)

Rnd 58: Knit to marker, SM, K1, (P1, K1) 6 times, SM, knit to end of rnd.

Rnd 59: Knit to marker, SM, P1, (K1, P1) 6 times, SM, knit to last st on needle tip, K1f&b, knit to last st of rnd, K1f&b. (53 sts)

Rnd 60: Knit to marker, SM, P1, (K1, P1) 6 times, SM, knit to end of rnd.

Rnd 61: K1f&b, knit to marker, SM, K1, (P1, K1) 6 times, SM, knit to end of needle tip, K1f&b, knit to end of rnd. (55 sts). Place removable markers in sts 1 and 29 to mark for legs.

Rnd 62: Knit to marker, SM, K1, (P1, K1) 6 times, SM, knit to end of rnd.

Rnd 63: Knit to marker, SM, P1, (K1, P1) 6 times, SM, knit to last st on needle tip, K1f&b, knit to last st of rnd, K1f&b. (57 sts)

Rnd 64: Knit to marker, SM, P1, (K1, P1) 6 times, SM, knit to end of rnd.

Rnd 65: K1f&b, knit to marker, SM, K1, (P1, K1) 6 times, SM, knit to end of needle tip, K1f&b, knit to end of rnd. (59 sts)

Rnd 66: Knit to marker, SM, K1, (P1, K1) 6 times, SM, knit to end of rnd.

Rnd 67: Knit to marker, SM, P1, (K1, P1) 6 times, SM, knit to last on needle tip, K1f&b, knit to last st of rnd, K1f&b. (61 sts)

Rnd 68: Knit to marker, SM, P1, (K1, P1) 6 times, SM, knit to end of rnd.

Rnd 69: K1f&b, knit to marker, SM, K1, (P1, K1) 6 times, SM, knit to end of needle tip, K1f&b, knit to end of rnd. (63 sts). Place removable markers in sts 32 and 63 to mark for legs.

Rnd 70: Knit to marker, SM, K1, (P1, K1) 6 times, SM, knit to end of rnd.

Rnd 71: Knit to marker, SM, P1, (K1, P1) 6 times, SM, knit to last st on needle tip, K1f&b, knit to last st of rnd, K1f&b. (65 sts)

Rnd 72: Knit to marker, SM, P1, (K1, P1) 6 times, SM, knit to end of rnd.

Rnd 73: Knit to marker, SM, K1, (P1, K1) 6 times, SM, knit to end of rnd.

Rnd 74: Knit to marker, SM, K1, (P1, K1) 6 times, SM, knit to end of rnd.

Rnd 75: Knit to marker, SM, P1, (K1, P1) 6 times, SM, knit to end of rnd.

Rnd 76–112: Rep rnds 72–75 another 9 times, then rep rnd 1 once more. Place removable markers as you work:

> **Rnd 98:** PM in sts 1 and 34 to mark for legs.

> **Rnd 106:** PM in sts 33 and 65 to mark for legs.

Rnd 113: Ssk, knit to marker, SM, work in patt to next marker, SM, knit to end of needle tip; on second needle tip, ssk, knit to end of rnd. (63 sts)

Rnds 114 and 115: Knit to marker, SM, work in patt to next marker, SM, knit to end of rnd.

Rnd 116: Knit to marker, SM, work in patt to next marker, SM, knit to last 2 sts on needle tip, K2tog; on second needle tip, knit to last 2 sts of rnd, K2tog. (61 sts)

Rnds 117 and 118: Knit to marker, SM, work in patt to next marker, SM, knit to end of rnd.

Rnd 119: Ssk, knit to marker, SM, work in patt to next marker, SM, knit to end of needle tip; on second needle tip, ssk, knit to end of rnd. (59 sts)

Rnds 120 and 121: Knit to marker, SM, work in patt to next marker, SM, knit to end of rnd.

Rnd 122: Knit to marker, SM, work in patt to next marker, SM, knit to last 2 sts on needle tip, K2tog; on second needle tip, knit to last 2 sts of rnd, K2tog. (57 sts)

Rnds 123 and 124: Knit to marker, SM, work in patt to next marker, SM, knit to end of rnd.

Rnd 125: Ssk, knit to marker, SM, work in patt to next marker, SM, knit to end of needle tip; on second needle tip, ssk, knit to end of rnd. (55 sts)

Rnd 126: Knit to marker, SM, work in patt to next marker, SM, knit to end of rnd.

Rnd 127: Knit to marker, remove marker, K1, PM, work in patt to last st before next marker, sl next st, remove marker, sl unworked st back to LH needle, PM, knit to end of rnd. (11 sts between markers)

Rnd 128: Knit to marker, SM, work in patt to next marker, SM, knit to last 2 sts on needle tip, K2tog; on second needle tip, knit to last 2 sts of rnd, K2tog. (53 sts)

Rnds 129 and 130: Knit to marker, SM, work in patt to next marker, SM, knit to end of rnd.

Rnd 131: Ssk, knit to marker, SM, work in patt to next marker, SM, knit to end of needle tip; on second needle tip, ssk, knit to end of rnd. (51 sts)

Rnds 132 and 133: Knit to marker, SM, work in patt to next marker, SM, knit to end of rnd.

Rnd 134: Knit to marker, SM, work in patt to next marker, SM, knit to last 2 sts on needle tip, K2tog; on second needle tip, knit to last 2 sts of rnd, K2tog. (49 sts)

Rnds 135 and 136: Knit to marker, SM, work in patt to second marker, SM, knit to end of rnd.

Rnd 137: Ssk, knit to marker, remove marker, K1, PM, work in patt to last st before next marker, sl next st, remove marker, sl unworked st back to LH needle, knit to end of needle tip; flip to second needle tip, ssk, knit to end of rnd. (47 sts, 9 sts between markers)

TAIL

STAR

Rnds 138 and 139: Knit to marker, SM, work in patt to second marker, SM, knit to end of rnd.

Rnd 140: Knit to marker, SM, work in patt to next marker, SM, knit to last 2 sts on needle tip, K2tog; on second needle tip, knit to last 2 sts of rnd, K2tog. (45 sts)

Rnds 141 and 142: Knit to marker, SM, work in patt to second marker, SM, knit to end of rnd.

Begin to stuff body. Add safety eyes.

Rnd 143: Ssk, knit to marker, remove marker, K1, PM, work in patt to last st before next marker, sl next st, remove marker, sl unworked st back to LH needle, knit to end of needle tip; flip to second needle tip, ssk, knit to end of rnd. (43 sts, 7 sts between markers)

Rnds 144 and 145: Knit to marker, SM, work in patt to second marker, SM, knit to end of rnd.

Rnd 146: Knit to marker, SM, work in patt to next marker, SM, knit to last 2 sts on needle tip, K2tog; on second needle tip, knit to last 2 sts of rnd, K2tog. (41 sts)

Rnds 147 and 148: Knit to marker, SM, work in patt to second marker, SM, knit to end of rnd.

Rnd 149: Ssk, knit to marker, SM, work in patt to next marker, SM, knit to end of needle tip; on second needle tip, ssk, knit to end of rnd. (39 sts)

Rnds 150 and 151: Knit to marker, SM, work in patt to second marker, SM, knit to end of rnd.

Rnd 152: Knit to marker, SM, work in patt to next marker, SM, knit to last 2 sts on needle tip, K2tog; on second needle tip, knit to last 2 sts of rnd, K2tog. (37 sts)

Rnds 153 and 154: Knit to marker, SM, work in patt to second marker, SM, knit to end of rnd.

Rnd 155: Ssk, knit to marker, SM, work in patt to next marker, SM, knit to end of needle tip; on second needle tip, ssk, knit to end of rnd. (35 sts)

Rnd 156: Knit to marker, SM, work in patt to second marker, SM, knit to end of rnd.

Rnd 157: Knit to marker, remove marker, K1, PM, work in patt to last st before next marker, sl next st, remove marker, sl unworked st back to left hand needle, PM, knit to end of rnd. (5 sts between markers). Add more stuffing to body now.

Rnd 158: Knit to marker, SM, work in patt to next marker, SM, knit to last 2 sts on needle tip, K2tog; on second needle tip, knit to last 2 sts of rnd, K2tog. (33 sts)

Rnds 159 and 160: Knit to marker, SM, work in patt to second marker, SM, knit to end of rnd.

KNIT SUPERHEROES!

Rnd 161: Ssk, knit to marker, SM, work in patt to next marker, SM, knit to end of needle tip; on second needle tip, ssk, knit to end of rnd. (31 sts)

Rnds 162 and 163: Knit to marker, SM, work in patt to second marker, SM, knit to end of rnd.

Rnd 164: Knit to marker, SM, work in patt to next marker, SM, knit to last 2 sts on needle tip, K2tog; on second needle tip, knit to last 2 sts of rnd, K2tog. (29 sts)

Rnds 165 and 166: Knit to marker, SM, work in patt to second marker, SM, knit to end of rnd.

Rnd 167: Ssk, knit to marker, remove marker, K1, PM, work in patt to last st before next marker, sl next st, remove marker, sl unworked st back to left hand needle, PM, knit to end of needle tip; flip to second needle tip, ssk, knit to end of rnd. (27 sts, 3 sts between markers)

Rnds 168 and 169: Knit to marker, SM, work in patt to second marker, SM, knit to end of rnd.

Rnd 170: Knit to marker, SM, work in patt to next marker, SM, knit to last 2 sts on needle tip, K2tog; on second needle tip, knit to last 2 sts of rnd, K2tog. (25 sts)

Rnds 171 and 172: Knit to marker, SM, work in patt to second marker, SM, knit to end of rnd.

Rnd 173: Knit to marker, remove marker, K2tog, K1, remove marker, knit to end of rnd. (24 sts)

Rnd 174: (K1, ssk, knit to last 3 sts on needle tip, K2tog, K1) twice. (20 sts)

Rnd 175: Knit all sts.

Rnd 176: (K1, ssk, knit to last 3 sts on needle tip, K2tog, K1) twice. (16 sts)

Rnd 177: Knit all sts.

Rnd 178: (K1, ssk, knit to last 3 sts on needle tip, K2tog, K1) twice. (12 sts)

Rnd 179: Knit all sts.

Add final stuffing.

Rnd 180: K2tog 6 times around. (6 sts)

Cut yarn and using a tapestry needle, pull tail through rem sts to close.

LEGS

Rnd 1: Using green and starting in marked st 1 on rnd 61, PU 9 sts, 1 st per rnd toward tail. Slide sts to cable to set up for magic loop method, and starting with marked st 32 from rnd 69 and heading in opposite direction, PU same 9 sts 1 st over. (18 sts). PM in first picked-up st of rnd to indicate beg of rnd.

Rnds 2–24: Knit all sts.

Rnd 25: (K1f&b, knit to last st on needle tip, K1f&b) twice. (22 sts)

Rnd 26: Knit all sts.

Rnds 27–32: Rep rnds 25 and 26. (34 sts)

Rnds 33–38: Knit all sts.

Rnd 39: (K1, ssk, knit to last 3 sts on needle tip, K2tog, K1) twice. (30 sts)

Rnd 40: Knit all sts.

Rnds 41–44: Rep rnds 39 and 40. (22 sts)

Rnds 45 and 46: Rep rnd 39. (14 sts)

Stuff foot. Cut yarn, leaving a generous tail and work Kitchener st to close.

Rep with marked sts on rnds 69, 98, and 106 for other 3 legs.

CAPE BAND, CAPE, AND STAR

All are knit flat (back and forth), not in the round.

BAND

Using black, CO 6 sts. DO NOT JOIN.

Knit every row (garter st) for 118 rows, placing removable markers on last st of rows 34 and 90.

Buttonhole row: K2, BO 2 sts, K2. (4 sts)

Finish buttonhole: K2, cable CO 2 sts, K2. (6 sts)

Knit 6 more rows in garter st.

Loosely BO all sts.

CAPE

Row 1 (set up): Using black and starting in marked st on row 34 of cape band, PU 28 sts, 1 st per garter ridge to marked st on row 90. (28 sts)

Rows 2–6: Knit every row (garter st) for 5 more rows.

Row 7: K1f&b, knit to end of row. (29 sts)

Rows 8–12: Knit all sts.

Row 13: Knit to last 2 sts, K1f&b, K1. (30 sts)

Rows 14–18: Knit all sts.

Rows 19–138: Rep rows 7–18 another 10 times. (50 sts)

Loosely BO all sts.

STAR

Using yellow and circular needle, CO 2 sts. DO NOT JOIN.

Row 1: K1f&b, K1. (3 sts)

Row 2 and all even-numbered rows: Knit all sts.

Row 3: K1f&b, knit to end of row. (4 sts)

Row 5: Knit to last 2 sts, K1f&b, K1. (5 sts)

Row 7: Rep row 3. (6 sts)

Row 9: Rep row 5. (7 sts)

Row 11: Rep row 3. (8 sts)

Rows 12–18: Knit all sts.

Cut yarn and place sts on spare circular needle.

Rep rows 1–12 to make 4 more points, placing each on your spare needle as you complete it. Leave working yarn attached on last point.

Join center of star as follows:

Row 1 (set up rnd): Knitting from spare needle to main needle, knit across all 5 points. Divide point sts in half for set-up to work in rnd using magic loop method. (40 sts). Join sts by knitting from last st worked (where working yarn is attached) to first st worked. Cont in the round using magic loop method.

Rnd 2: Purl all sts.

Rnd 3: Knit all sts.

Rnd 4: (P2tog, P3) around. (32 sts)

Rnd 5: Knit all sts.

Rnd 6: (P2tog, P2) around. (24 sts)

Rnd 7: Knit all sts.

Rnd 8: (P2tog, P1) around. (16 sts)

Rnd 9: Knit all sts.

Rnd 10: P2tog around. (8 sts)

Cut yarn and using a tapestry needle, pull tail through rem sts to close up star.

FINISH ALBERTO

Weave in rem ends. Pin star to center of cape and use yellow yarn and running st to sew in place. Using sewing needle and thread, place button on band to match up with buttonhole, and sew button in place. Tah-dah! Now go put on some Elvis music and get to impersonating!

HEROIC HERSCHEL

• HAPPENSTANCE HIPPO •

Being a superhero hippo can be a tough job. Hippos are not particularly agile or skilled in the areas of most superheroes. **LUCKY FOR HERSCHEL, HIS SUPERPOWER LIES IN BEING AT THE RIGHT PLACE AT THE RIGHT TIME.** Though not exceptionally sprightly, he can generally just use his large size to stop whatever super villain is around. Especially if he sits on top of them.

SAMPLES

COBASI SOCK YARN (below)

* Approx 11" from head to toe
* Colors: Deep Turquoise 010, Carrot 070, Butter Cream 042
* 9 mm black safety eyes

MERINO WORSTED (page 56)

* Approx 14" from head to toe
* Colors: Lagoon, Tangerine, Zest
* 15 mm black safety eyes

MATERIALS

YARN

Turquoise: 180–215 yds for hippo

Orange: 125–180 yds for shorts and cape

Yellow: 90–130 yds for shorts and cape

Waste yarn for holding live sts

Black scrap yarn for nostrils

NEEDLES

36" or longer circular needle in a size 2 or 3 sizes smaller than those recommended for your yarn (for magic loop method)

3 double-pointed needles in same size as circular needle for tail

NOTIONS

Basic supplies (see "What to Keep in Your Utility Belt" on page 12)

7 removable st markers (or 6 removable st markers and 1 fixed marker)

2 safety eyes (see "Samples" for sizes)

LEGS AND BODY

Using turquoise, and referring to "Two-at-a-Time Legs" (page 13), CO 4 sts per leg.

Rnd 1: K1f&b in all sts. (8 sts each leg)

Rnd 2: Knit all sts.

Rnd 3: K1f&b in all sts. (16 sts each leg)

Rnd 4: Knit all sts.

Rnd 5: (K1f&b, K1) around. (24 sts each leg)

Rnds 6–28: Knit all sts.

Rnd 29: K11, K1f&b in last st from leg 1, K1f&b in first st of leg 2, knit to last st of leg 2, K1f&b, K1f&b in next st from leg 1, knit to end of rnd. (26 sts each leg)

Rnd 30: Knit all sts.

Rnd 31: K12, K1f&b in last st from leg 1, K1f&b in first st of leg 2, knit to last st of leg 2, K1f&b, K1f&b in next st from leg 1, knit to end of rnd. (28 sts each leg)

Rnd 32: K14 sts of leg 1, use knitted CO to CO 12 sts, cont with yarn from leg 1 for rest of rnd, knit across all 28 sts of leg 2, then use knitted CO to CO 12 sts, knit final 14 sts of rnd, cut yarn from leg 2. (80 sts). (Stuffing, eyes, and belly button will be added later through hole created here.)

Beg body.

Rnds 33–80: Knit all sts. Place removable markers as you work:

> **Rnd 52:** PM in sts 59 and 62 to mark for tail.

> **Rnd 76:** PM in sts 4, 37, 44, and 77 to mark for arms.

Rnd 81: (Ssk, knit to end of needle tip) twice. (78 sts)

Rnd 82: Knit all sts.

Rnd 83: (Knit to last 2 sts on needle tip, K2tog) twice. (76 sts)

Rnd 84: Knit all sts.

Rnds 85–87: Rep rnds 81–83. (72 sts)

Rnd 88 (place nose): K8, with waste yarn knit next 20 sts, slip waste yarn sts back to LH needle, go back to working yarn, knit to end of rnd.

Rnds 89–108: Rep rnds 81–84. (52 sts)

Rnd 109: (Ssk, knit to last 2 sts on needle tip, K2tog) twice. (48 sts). Place removable marker in sts 1 and 25 to mark for ears.

Rnds 110–113: Rep rnd 109. Do not PM. (32 sts)

Cut yarn, leaving a generous tail and work Kitchener st to close.

NOSE

Rnd 1: Using turquoise and first needle tip, PU right leg of the 20 sts along bottom of waste yarn on rnd 88, flip body so top of waste yarn is facing you and rep process using second needle tip. (40 sts). Using a tapestry needle, remove waste yarn, *PU 1 st before st on first needle tip, work across sts on first needle tip, PU 1 more st at end of needle tip; rep from * on second needle tip. (44 sts). Cont to work nose using magic loop method.

Rnd 2: (K1f&b, knit to last st on needle tip, K1f&b) twice. (48 sts)

Rnd 3: Rep rnd 2. (52 sts)

Rnds 4–23: Knit all sts.

Rnd 24: (Ssk, knit to last 2 sts on needle tip, K2tog) twice. (48 sts)

Rnds 25–28: Rep rnd 24. (32 sts)

Cut yarn, leaving a generous tail and work Kitchener st to close.

FACE

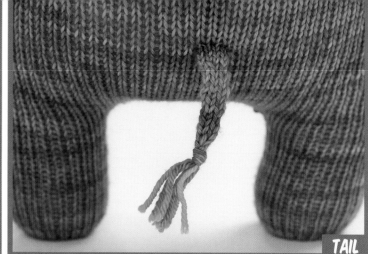

TAIL

EARS

Rnd 1: Using turquoise and starting in marked st 1 on rnd 109, PU 4 sts, 1 st per rnd toward top of head. Slide sts to cable to set up for magic loop method and heading in opposite direction, move 1 st toward back of head and PU same 4 sts. (8 sts). PM in first picked-up st of rnd to indicate beg of rnd.

Rnds 2 and 3: Knit all sts.

Rnd 4: (K1f&b, K3) twice. (10 sts)

Rnd 5: (K4, K1f&b) twice. (12 sts)

Rnd 6: (K2, K1f&b, K3) twice. (14 sts)

Rnds 7–12: Knit all sts.

Rnd 13: (K2tog) around. (7 sts)

Stuff ear as desired (samples' ears are unstuffed). Cut yarn and using a tapestry needle, pull tail through rem sts to close ear.

Rep with marked st 25 on rnd 109 to make other ear.

ARMS

Rnd 1: Using turquoise and starting in marked st 77 on rnd 76, PU 8 sts, 1 per st to marker to st 4. Slide sts to cable to set up for magic loop method and heading in opposite direction, PU same 8 sts 1 rnd up. (16 sts). PM in first picked-up st of rnd to indicate beg of rnd.

Rnds 2–14: Knit all sts.

Rnd 15: (K1f&b, knit to end of needle tip) twice. (18 sts)

Rnds 16 and 17: Knit all sts.

Rnd 18: (Knit to last st on needle tip, K1f&b) twice. (20 sts)

Rnds 19 and 20: Knit all sts.

Rnds 21–26: Rep rnds 15–20. (24 sts)

Rnds 27–44: Knit all sts.

Rnd 45: (K2tog) around. (12 sts)

Stuff arm. Cut yarn and using a tapestry needle, pull tail through rem sts to close.

Rep with marked sts 37 and 44 on rnd 76 for other arm.

TAIL

Rnd 1: Using turquoise and a dpn, start in marked st 61 on rnd 52, and PU 4 sts, 1 per st to marked st 58. Using a second dpn, and heading in opposite direction, PU same 4 sts 1 rnd up. (8 sts). PM in first picked-up st of rnd to indicate beg of rnd.

Rnds 2–4: Knit all sts.

Rnd 5: (Ssk, K2) twice. (6 sts)

Work I-cord (see page 92) to end of tail.

Rnds 6–8: Knit all sts.

KNIT SUPERHEROES!

Rnd 9: K2, K2tog, K2. (5 sts)

Rnds 10 and 11: Knit all sts.

Rnd 12: K1, K2tog, K2. (4 sts)

Rnds 13 and 14: Knit all sts.

Rnd 15: (K2tog) twice. (2 sts)

Cut yarn and pull through rem sts. Cut 6 pieces of turquoise, 6" long, for fringe. Holding 6 strands tog, add fringe to end of tail and tie end in a knot. Trim ends of fringe even, about ¾" long.

CAPE BAND AND CAPE

Both are knit flat (back and forth), not in the round.

BAND

Using orange, CO 6 sts. DO NOT JOIN.

Knit every row (garter st) for 258 rows, placing removable markers on last st of rows 90 and 168.

2-COLOR SUPERSTAR PATTERN

Row 1: With yellow, K2, (YO, K3, pass first of 3 knit sts over 2nd and 3rd sts); rep across row to last st, K1.

Row 2: With yellow, purl all sts.

Row 3: With orange, K1, (K3, pass first of 3 knit sts over 2nd and 3rd sts, YO); rep across row to last 2 sts, K2.

Row 4: With orange, purl all sts.

CAPE

Set-up row: Using yellow and starting in marked st on row 90 of cape band, PU 39 sts, 1 st per garter ridge to marked st on row 168. (39 sts). Cont to knit back and forth to finish cape.

Inc row: Cont with yellow, K1f&b 39 times. (78 sts)

Rows 1–76: Work rows 1–4 of superstar patt a total of 19 times. (38 stripes)

59

Rows 77 and 78: Work rows 1 and 2 of superstar patt once more. (39 stripes)

Rows 79 and 80: With orange, knit all sts (garter st).

Loosely BO all sts.

SUPER SHORTS

Using orange and circular needle, CO 88 sts. PM to indicate beg of rnd and beg to work in rnd using magic loop method.

Rnds 1–4: (K2, P2) around.

Rnds 5–32: With yellow, knit all sts in est stripe patt of 4 rnds yellow, 4 rnds orange.

Rnd 33: With orange, K31, BO 26 sts, K18, BO 26 sts (starting in rnd 33 and ending in next rnd). (36 sts rem)

Leaving sts that are not attached to working yarn on cable of needle, work sts attached to working yarn back and forth in St st. Work 3 rows in orange to complete a 4-row orange stripe. Work 4 rows in yellow, then work 2 rows in orange. Cut yarn. Do not BO.

Join orange to opposite live sts that have been on cable. Work same stripe patt as other side in St st, 3 rows orange, 4 rows yellow, 2 rows orange. Cut yarn, leaving a long tail. Bring sts tog and work Kitchener st to close shorts.

Finish leg openings as follows:

Rnd 1: Using orange and circular needle, PU 44 sts around leg opening.

Rnds 2 and 3: (K2, P2) around.

Loosely BO all sts in patt. Rep for other leg opening.

NOTE ON SHORTS

I made the shorts to fit my rotund hippos. If your hippo comes out skinnier and your shorts are too big, simply run a piece of yarn through the waistband and make them drawstring shorts.

FINISH HERSCHEL

Weave in rem ends. Block cape as desired. Stuff body and add safety eyes. Using scrap black yarn and tapestry needle, stitch an X on Herschel's tummy to make a belly button. Tie ends off inside of tummy. Use a whipstitch to close hole between Herschel's legs. Slip on Herschel's shorts, tie on his cape, and go fight some crime.

HARRY ELEFANTE

• LOUNGE SINGER EXTRAORDINAIRE •

Harry Elefante is an international lounge singer superstar who is booked solid for the next three years. When Harry is not jet-setting to his next gig, HE HAS A SECRET SUPERPOWER HE USES TO KEEP CRIMINALS AT BAY. He is the most charming and funny guy you have ever met—he can charm anyone into doing anything he wants, just by talking to them. The police love Harry, since he simply talks marauders and gangsters into turning themselves in and confessing everything.

SAMPLES

COBASI SOCK YARN (below)

* Approx 11" from face to tail, 7" from head to toe, not including trunk
* Colors: Gun Metal Grey 037, Raffi 051, Royal 029
* 9 mm black safety eyes

MERINO WORSTED (page 62)

* Approx 16" from face to tail, 10" from head to toe, not including trunk
* Colors: Foil, Navy, Pool
* 15 mm black safety eyes

MATERIALS

YARN

Gray: 200–300 yds for elephant

Dark Blue: 30–50 yds for utility belt and leg bands

Light Blue: 70–100 yds for utility belt

Waste yarn for holding live sts

NEEDLES

36" or longer circular needle in a size 2 or 3 sizes smaller than those recommended for your yarn (for magic loop method)

2 double-pointed needles in same size for I-cord

NOTIONS

Basic supplies (see "What to Keep in Your Utility Belt" on page 12)

7 removable st markers (or 6 removable st markers and 1 fixed marker)

2 safety eyes (see "Samples" for sizes)

BODY AND LEGS

Harry is worked from rump to trunk.

Using gray and Turkish CO (page 93), wrap 52 loops (for 104 sts) onto circular needle. PM to indicate beg of rnd and beg body using magic loop method.

Rnd 1: Knit loops from Turkish CO to beg working in the round.

Rnd 2: (K1f&b, knit to last st on needle tip, K1f&b) twice. (108 sts)

Rnd 3: Knit all sts.

Rnds 4–17: Rep rnds 2 and 3. (136 sts). Place removable markers as you work:

> **Rnd 16:** PM in sts 49 and 68 to mark for ears.

> **Rnd 17:** PM in st 1 to mark for tail.

Rnds 18–44: Knit all sts. Place removable markers as you work:

> **Rnd 40:** PM in sts 54 and 83 to mark for ears.

Rnd 45: K58, place next 20 sts on waste yarn for trunk, knit to end of rnd. (116 sts)

Rnds 46–57: Knit all sts.

LEG 1

Rnd 1: K9, place next 98 sts on waste yarn. Bring yarn across gap and knit last 9 sts of rnd. (18 sts)

Rnds 2–17: Knit all sts.

Rnd 18: (Ssk, K5, K2tog) twice. (14 sts)

Cut yarn, leaving a generous tail and work Kitchener st to close.

Place next 5 sts and last 5 sts from waste yarn onto needle for 10 total sts on needles. Join in a length of yarn and work Kitchener st to close these 10 sts between legs.

LEG 2

Place first 9 sts and last 9 sts from waste yarn onto needle for 18 sts on needles.

Rnd 1: Join in working yarn and knit all sts.

Rnds 2–17: Knit all sts.

Rnd 18: (Ssk, K5, K2tog) twice. (14 sts)

Cut yarn, leaving a generous tail and work Kitchener st to close.

Place next 12 sts and last 12 sts from waste yarn onto a 2nd piece of waste yarn for 24 total sts on new waste yarn. You'll leave these sts live for stuffing through this hole and finishing later.

LEG 3

Place first 9 sts and last 9 sts from original waste yarn onto needle for 18 sts on needles. Work leg 3 as you did leg 2.

Place next 5 sts and last 5 sts from waste yarn onto needle for 10 sts on needles. Join in a length of yarn and work Kitchener st to close these 10 sts as you did between legs 1 and 2.

LEG 4

Place rem 18 sts from waste yarn on needles and work as for other 3 legs.

TRUNK

Place 20 held trunk sts on needles so beg of rnd is on body side.

Rnd 1: PU 1 st from body/trunk gap, knit all sts, PU 1 additional st from body/trunk gap. (22 sts)

Rnds 2–4: Knit all sts.

Rnd 5: Ssk, knit to end of rnd. (21 sts)

Rnds 6–14: Knit all sts.

Rnd 15: Knit to last 2 sts, K2tog. (20 sts)

Rnds 16–24: Knit all sts.

Rnds 25–44: Rep rnds 5–24. (18 sts)

Rnds 45–65: Knit all sts.

Rnd 66: (Ssk, K5, K2tog) twice. 14 sts.

Cut yarn, leaving a generous tail and work Kitchener st to close.

TAIL

Rnd 1: Using gray and a dpn, beg in marked st 1 from rnd 17, and PU 4 sts in a square. Cont by knitting these sts as an I-cord (see page 92).

Rnds 2–20: Knit all sts.

Cut yarn and use a tapestry needle to pull tail through rem sts to close tail. Cut 6 pieces of gray, 6" long, for fringe. Holding all 6 strands tog, attach fringe on base of tail. Tie in a knot and trim ends even to about ¾".

EARS

Rnd 1: Using gray and starting in marked st 54 on rnd 40, PU 24 sts, 2 sts picked up for every 3 rnds. (Knit fabric is longer than it is wide, so this ratio is needed for ear to lie flat, not bunch.) Slide sts to cable to set up for magic loop method and starting with marker in st 49 from rnd 6, PU same 24 sts 1 st over. (48 sts). PM in first picked-up st of rnd to indicate beg of rnd.

Rnd 2: (K1f&b, knit to last st of needle tip, K1f&b) twice. (52 sts)

Rnd 3: Knit all sts.

Rnd 4: Rep rnd 2. (56 sts)

Rnds 5–18: Knit all sts.

Rnd 19: (K1, ssk, knit to last 3 sts on needle tip, K2tog, K1) twice. (52 sts)

Rnd 20: Knit all sts.

Rnds 21 and 22: Rep rnds 19 and 20. (48 sts)

Rnds 23–25: Rep rnd 19. (36 sts)

Stuff ear if desired (samples' ears are unstuffed). Cut yarn, leaving a generous tail and work Kitchener st to close.

Rep with marked sts on rnds 40 and 6 to make other ear.

Stuff Harry and add his safety eyes. Slip held sts on waste yarn to needles. Join in a piece of yarn to one side of live sts on waste yarn, and work Kitchener st to close tummy.

LEG BANDS

Make 4.

Using dark blue and circular needle, CO 20 sts. PM to indicate beg of rnd and beg band using magic loop method.

Rnds 1–5: (K2, P2) around.

Loosely BO in patt.

UTILITY BELT

Using dark blue and circular needle, CO 96 sts. PM to indicate beg of rnd and beg belt using magic loop method.

Rnd 1: (K2, P2) around. Place removable markers on CO edge below sts 5, 23, 41, 59, and 77 to mark for pockets.

Rnds 2 and 3: With light blue, (K2, P2) around.

Rnds 4 and 5: With dark blue, (K2, P2) around.

KNIT SUPERHEROES!

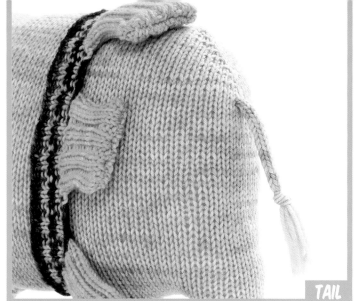

TAIL

BELT

Rnds 6 and 7: With light blue, (K2, P2) around.

Rnds 8 and 9: With dark blue, (K2, P2) around.

With dark blue, loosely BO in patt.

POCKETS

Pockets are knit in the same color, either light or dark blue.

POCKET 1

Rnd 1: Using circular needle, start with marked st 5, PU 16 sts, 1 st per st on belt, cable CO 16 sts. (32 sts). Slide sts to cable and set up for working in rnd using magic loop method.

Rnds 2–24: (K2, P2) around.

Turn pocket WS out and use 3-needle BO to close sts.

POCKET 2

Rnd 1: Starting with marked st 23, PU sts and CO sts as you did for pocket 1. (32 sts). Make sure pocket opens in same direction as pocket 1.

Rnds 2–16: (K2, P2) around.

Turn pocket WS out and use 3-needle BO to close sts.

POCKET 3

Rnd 1: Starting with marked st 41, PU sts and CO as you did for pockets 1 and 2. (32 sts)

Rnds 2–20: (K2, P2) around.

Turn pocket WS out and use 3-needle BO to close sts.

POCKET 4

Starting with marked st 59, work as for pocket 2.

POCKET 5

Starting with marked st 77, work as for pocket 1.

FINISH HARRY

Weave in rem ends. Whipstitch shut any holes created from holding sts. Block utility belt as desired. Put leg bands on legs, utility belt around his middle, and fill his pockets with crime-fighting tools (like a microphone and some gum). Now he is ready for charming those bandits!

THE BLACK SQUIRRELLY

• MASTER STEALTH NINJA •

THE BLACK SQUIRRELLY IS A JUJITSU MASTER and has been studying with the most famous and influential squirrel martial-arts masters in the world, since he was a wee baby squirrel. He spends all day training, sneaking along power lines and tops of fences to pounce upon and grapple with unsuspecting acorns and pinecones. His dark fur makes him almost ninja like, and all the creatures in his neighborhood know they can rely on him for protection.

SAMPLES

COBASI SOCK YARN (below)

* Approx 11" from head to toe
* Colors: Black 002, Really Red 047, Gun Metal Grey 037
* 9 mm black safety eyes
* ⅝"-diameter button
* 1 ball of Romance from Lion Brand Yarns (84% nylon, 16% polyester; 1.75 oz/50 g; 27 yds/ 27 m) in Moonlight

MERINO WORSTED (at right)

* Approx 18" from head to toe
* Colors: Casting Shadows, Pomegranate, Foil
* 15 mm black safety eyes
* 1⅛"-diameter button
* 1 ball of Romance from Lion Brand Yarns in Moonlight

MATERIALS

YARN

Black: 115–165 yds for body

Red: 50–80 yds for sweater and utility belt

Gray: 45–75 yds for mask and sweater

Black Eyelash: 20–25 yds for tail

NEEDLES

36" or longer circular needle in a size 2 or 3 sizes smaller than those recommended for your yarn (for magic loop method)

2 double-pointed needles in same size as circular needle for I-cord

NOTIONS

Basic supplies (see "What to Keep in Your Utility Belt" on page 12)

13 removable st markers (or 11 removable st markers and 2 fixed markers)

2 safety eyes (see "Samples" for sizes)

1 button to close utility belt (see "Samples" for sizes)

Sewing needle and thread to attach button

BODY

Squirrelly begins at base of body.

Using black and circular needle, CO 4 sts. PM to indicate beg of rnd and beg body using magic loop method.

Rnd 1: K1f&b 4 times. (8 sts)

Rnd 2: Knit all sts.

Rnd 3: K1f&b 8 times. (16 sts)

Rnd 4: Knit all sts.

Rnd 5: (K1f&b, K1) around. (24 sts)

Rnd 6: Knit all sts. Place removable markers in sts 1 and 13 to mark for legs.

Rnd 7: (K1f&b, K2) around. (32 sts)

Rnd 8: Knit all sts.

Rnd 9: (K1f&b, K3) around. (40 sts)

Rnd 10: Knit all sts.

Rnd 11: (K1f&b, K4) around. (48 sts)

Rnd 12: Knit all sts.

Rnd 13: (K1f&b, K5) around. (56 sts)

Rnd 14: Knit all sts.

Rnd 15: (K1f&b, K6) around. (64 sts)

Rnd 16: Knit all sts.

Rnd 17: (K1f&b, K7) around. (72 sts)

Rnds 18–26: Knit all sts. After rnd 26, place removable markers in sts 49 and 60 to mark for tail.

Rnds 27–30: With gray, knit all sts.

Rnds 31–60: Knit all sts in stripe patt of 2 rnds red, 3 rnds gray, ending with gray stripe. Place removable markers as you work:

> **Rnd 57:** PM in sts 3, 34, 39, and 70 to mark for arms.

Rnd 61: With gray, knit all sts.

Rnd 62: With black, knit all sts. Cont in black to top of head.

Rnd 63: K2tog 36 times. (36 sts)

Rnds 64–66: Knit all sts.

Rnd 67: (K1f&b, K2) around. (48 sts)

Rnd 68: Knit all sts.

Rnd 69: K12, PM, knit to end of rnd.

Rnd 70: Knit to 1 st before marker, K1f&b, SM, K1f&b, knit to end of rnd. (50 sts)

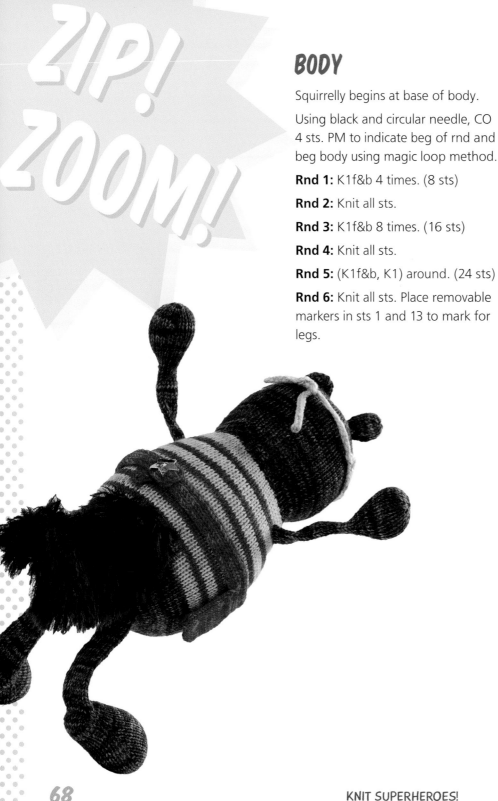

Rnd 71: Knit all sts.

Rnds 72–81: Rep rnds 70 and 71. (60 sts). After rnd 81, place removable marker in st 18 to mark for nose.

Rnd 82: Knit all sts.

Rnd 83: Knit to 3 sts before marker, ssk, K1, SM, K1, K2tog, knit to end of rnd. (58 sts)

Rnd 84: Knit all sts.

Rnds 85–94: Rep rnds 83 and 84. (48 sts)

Rnds 95–98: Knit all sts. After rnd 98, place removable markers in sts 1 and 25 to mark for ears.

Rnd 99: (K2tog, K2) around. (36 sts)

Rnd 100: Knit all sts.

Rnd 101: (K2tog, K1) around. (24 sts)

Rnd 102: Knit all sts.

Stuff body. Add safety eyes.

Rnd 103: K2tog around. (12 sts)

Rnd 104: Knit all sts.

Rnd 105: K2tog around. (6 sts)

Finish stuffing. Cut yarn and using a tapestry needle, pull tail through rem sts to close.

ARMS

Rnd 1: Using black and starting in marked st 70 on rnd 57, PU 6 sts, 1 per st toward marked st 3. Slide sts to cable to set up for magic loop method and heading in opposite direction, PU same 6 sts 1 rnd up. (12 sts). Be sure beg of rnd is to back of body for correct paw shaping, PM.

Rnds 2–30: Knit all sts.

Rnd 31: K1f&b 6 times, K6. (18 sts)

Rnds 32–42: Knit all sts.

Rnd 43: K2tog 6 times, K6. (12 sts)

Rnd 44: Knit all sts.

Rnd 45: K2tog around. (6 sts)

Stuff hand. Cut yarn and using a tapestry needle, pull tail through rem sts to close.

Rep with marked sts 39 and 70 on rnd 57 to make other arm.

LEGS

Rnd 1: Using black and starting in marked st 1 on rnd 6, PU 8 sts, 1 per purl bump inc and 1 in the st next to it, moving toward outside of body. Slide sts to cable to set up for magic loop method, move 1 st toward front of body and heading in opposite direction, PU same 8 sts. (16 sts). Be sure beg of rnd is toward back of body to ensure correct heel placement, PM.

Rnds 2–35: Knit all sts.

Work heel back and forth on first 8 sts of rnd, holding last 8 sts of rnd on cable.

Row 1: Sl 1, knit to end. Turn.

Row 2: Sl 1, purl to end. Turn.

Rows 3–8: Rep rows 1 and 2.

WORK FOOT

Rnd 1: Knit across 8 heel sts again. Using same needle tip, PU 5 sts from gusset edge. Slide sts to cable to set up for magic loop method and knit 8 held sts. Using same needle tip, PU 5 sts from gusset edge. (26 sts). PM in next st to be knitted to indicate beg of rnd.

Rnd 2: K8, PM, (K2tog) twice, K10 to last 4 sts, (ssk) twice. (22 sts)

Rnd 3: Knit all sts.

Rnd 4: Knit to marker, SM, K2tog, knit to last 2 sts, ssk. (20 sts)

Rnds 5–7: Knit all sts.

Rnd 8: Knit to marker, SM, K1f&b, knit to last st, K1f&b. (22 sts)

Rnd 9: Knit all sts.

Rnds 10–19: Rep rnds 8 and 9 another 5 times. (32 sts)

Rnds 20–22: Knit all sts.

Rnd 23: K2tog around, removing markers as you go. (16 sts)

Rnd 24: Knit all sts.

Rnd 25: K2tog around. (8 sts)

Stuff foot. Cut yarn and using a tapestry needle, pull tail through rem sts to close.

Rep with marked st 13 on rnd 6 to make other leg.

TAIL

Make sure to use a row counter here as it is nearly impossible to count how many rounds you have knit in the eyelash yarn.

Rnd 1: Using black eyelash and starting in marked st 49 on rnd 26, PU 12 sts, 1 per st to marked st 60. Slide sts to cable to set up for magic loop method and heading in opposite direction, PU same 12 sts 1 row up. (24 sts). PM in first picked-up st of rnd to indicate beg of rnd.

Rnd 2: (K1f&b, K10, K1f&b) twice. (28 sts)

Rnds 3–40: Knit all sts.

Rnd 41: (K2, K2tog 6 times) twice. (16 sts)

Rnd 42: Knit all sts.

Rnd 43: K2tog around. (8 sts)

Cut yarn and using a tapestry needle, pull tail through rem sts to close.

EARS

Rnd 1: Using black and starting in marked st 1 on rnd 98, PU 4 sts, 1 st per rnd toward top of head. Slide sts to cable to set up for magic loop method and heading in opposite direction, PU same 4 sts down back of head. (8 sts). PM in first picked-up st of rnd to indicate beg of rnd.

Rnd 2: (K1f&b, knit to last st on needle tip, K1f&b) twice. (12 sts)

Rnd 3: Knit all sts.

Rnds 4 and 5: Rep rnds 2 and 3. (16 sts)

Rnds 6–10: Knit all sts.

Rnd 11: K2tog around. (8 sts)

Stuff ear if desired (samples' ears are unstuffed). Cut yarn and using a tapestry needle, pull tail through rem sts to close.

Rep with marked st 25 on rnd 98 for other ear.

NOSE

Rnd 1: Using gray and starting in marked st 18 on rnd 81, PU 2 sts. Slide sts to cable to set up for magic loop method and heading in opposite direction, PU same 2 sts 1 rnd up. (4 sts). PM in first picked-up st of rnd to indicate beg of rnd.

Rnd 2: K1f&b in all sts. (8 sts)

Rnd 3: Knit all sts.

Rnd 4: (K1f&b, K1) around. (12 sts)

Rnds 5 and 6: Knit all sts.

Stuff with a small amount of stuffing, or yarn scraps.

Rnd 7: K2tog around. (6 sts)

Cut yarn and using a tapestry needle, pull tail through rem sts to close.

UTILITY BELT

You can adjust the length of the belt to fit your Squirrelly. Just measure as you go and stop when it fits, making sure to include overlap for button.

Using red and circular needle, CO 8 sts. DO NOT JOIN.

Rows 1–4: (K2, P2) across.

Row 5 (buttonhole): K2, P1, BO 2 sts, K1, P2. (6 sts)

Row 6 (buttonhole): K2, P1, use knitted CO to CO 2 sts, K2, P2. (8 sts)

Rows 7–130: (K2, P2) across. Place removable markers as you work:

> **Row 40:** PM in last st to mark for pocket.

> **Row 80:** PM in last st to mark for pocket (same side as first marker).

Loosely BO all sts.

POCKETS

Make 2.

Rnd 1: Using red and starting with marked st on row 80, and moving away from center of belt, PU 10 sts, 1 per st on belt, then cable CO 10 sts. (20 sts). Find center of sts and set up to work in rnd using magic loop method.

Rnds 2–16: Knit all sts.

Turn pocket WS out and use 3-needle BO to BO all sts.

FACE

BELT

Rep with marked st on row 40, this time picking up toward center of belt and other pocket to make second pocket. Be sure pockets open on same side and adjust if necessary.

MASK AND TIES

Both are knit flat (back and forth), not in the round.

MASK

Using gray, CO 24 sts. DO NOT JOIN.

Row 1: Knit all sts

Row 2: Purl all sts.

Row 3: K1, K1f&b, knit to last 2 sts, K1f&b, K1. (26 sts)

Row 4: Purl all sts.

Rows 5 and 6: Rep rows 3 and 4. (28 sts)

Row 7: K1, K1f&b, K4, BO 6 sts, K3, BO 6 sts, K3, K1f&b, K1. (18 sts)

Row 8: P7, use knitted CO to CO 6 sts, P4, use knitted CO to CO 6 sts, purl to end of row. (30 sts)

Row 9: K1, ssk, knit to last 3 sts, K2tog, K1. (28 sts)

Row 10: Purl all sts.

Divide for mask shaping.

Row 11: K1, ssk, K8, K2tog, K1. Turn. (12 sts)

Row 12: P1, P2tog, P6, P2tog tbl, P1. Turn. (10 sts)

Row 13: K1, ssk, K4, K2tog, K1. Turn. (8 sts)

Row 14: P2tog 4 times. Turn. (4 sts)

Row 15: BO all sts. Cut yarn.

Join in yarn to rem sts, and rep rows 11–15 for other side.

TIES

Using gray and a dpn, PU 2 sts at top corner of mask. Work tie as an I-cord (see page 92).

Rnds 1–35: Knit all sts.

Cut yarn and using a tapestry needle, pull tail through rem sts to close.

Rep on opposite top corner of mask to make second tie.

FINISH SQUIRRELLY

Weave in ends. Block mask as desired. Place button on non-buttonhole end of utility belt to match up with buttonhole, and use needle and thread to sew in place. Slide on the utility belt, tie on the mask, and sneak up on some bad guys!

TIBERIUS TIGER
• TOTAL TRANSGRESSOR TAMER •

TIBERIUS TIGER IS A MASTERFUL CAMOUFLAGE EXPERT. Or at least he thinks he is. Unfortunately he's not, but he does manage to stop most criminals in their tracks. It's hard to focus on much else when there's a large tiger in the room pretending he is invisible. Since he's largely successful in his efforts, this only reinforces his belief that he can camouflage himself anywhere, which allows him to carry on with full invisibility confidence in his hero work.

SAMPLES

COBASI SOCK YARN (below)

* Approx 14" from ears to toes
* Colors: Carrot 070, Black 002, Natural 003, Deep Turquoise 010, Seafoam 101
* 9 mm black safety eyes or embroidered eyes

MERINO WORSTED (at right)

* Approx 19" from ears to toes
* Colors: Tangerine, Licorice, Natural, Lagoon, Zest
* 15 mm black safety eyes or embroidered eyes

MATERIALS

YARN

Orange: 150–200 yds for tiger

Black: 30–50 yds for tiger

White: 30–50 yds for face

Turquoise: 250–300 yds for mask and cape

Aqua or Yellow: 40–60 yds for lightning bolt

Scrap of black yarn for embroidering face

NEEDLES

36" or longer circular needle in a size 2 or 3 sizes smaller than those recommended for your yarn (for magic loop method)

NOTIONS

Basic supplies (see "What to Keep in Your Utility Belt" on page 12)

9 removable st markers (or 8 removable st markers and 1 fixed marker)

2 safety eyes (see "Samples" for sizes)

LEGS AND BODY

Using orange, and referring to "Two-at-a-Time Legs" (page 13), CO 6 sts per leg.

Rnd 1: With orange, K1f&b around. (12 sts each leg)

Rnd 2: Knit all sts.

Rnd 3: K1f&b around. (24 sts each leg)

Rnds 4–10: Knit all sts.

Rnds 11 and 12: With black, knit all sts.

Rnds 13–18: With orange, knit 4 rnds, then cont in est stripe patt of 4 rnds orange, 2 rnds black.

Rnd 19: With orange, K12 sts of leg 1, use knitted CO to CO 16 sts, cont with yarn from leg 1 for rest of rnd, knit across all 24 sts of leg 2, use knitted CO to CO 16 sts, knit final 12 sts of rnd. Cut yarn from leg 2. (80 sts). (Stuffing and safety eyes will be added through hole created here later.)

Begin body.

Rnds 20–22: With orange, knit all sts.

Rnds 23–42: With black, knit 2 rnds, then cont in est patt of 4 rnds orange, 2 rnds black. Place removable markers as you work:

> **Rnd 41:** PM in sts 57 and 64 to mark for tail.

Rnd 43: (Ssk, knit to end of needle tip) twice. (78 sts)

Rnds 44 and 45: Knit all sts.

Rnd 46: (Knit to last 2 sts on needle tip, K2tog) twice. (76 sts)

Rnds 47 and 48: Knit all sts.

Rnds 49–90: Rep rnds 43–48. (48 sts)

Rnd 91: (Ssk, K22) twice. (46 sts) Place removable markers in sts 5, 19, 28, and 42 to mark for arms.

Rnds 92–96: Rep rnds 44–48. (44 sts)

Rnds 97–102: Rep rnds 43–48. (40 sts)

Rnd 103: (K2tog, K3) 8 times. (32 sts)

Rnds 104–106: Knit all sts.

Rnd 107: (K1f&b, K1) around. (48 sts)

Rnd 108: Knit all sts.

Rnd 109: (K1f&b, knit to last st on needle tip, K1f&b) twice. (52 sts)

Rnd 110: Knit all sts.

Rnds 111–116: Rep rnds 109 and 110 another 3 times. (64 sts)

Rnds 117–138: Knit all sts. After rnd 138, place removable markers in sts 1 and 32 to mark for ears.

Rnd 139: (K2tog, K6) around. (56 sts)

Rnd 140: Knit all sts.

Rnd 141: (K2tog, K5) around. (48 sts)

Rnd 142: Knit all sts.

Rnd 143: (K2tog, K4) around. (40 sts)

Rnd 144: Knit all sts.

Rnd 145: (K2tog, K3) around. (32 sts)

Rnd 146: Knit all sts.

Rnd 147: (K2tog, K2) around. (24 sts)

Cut yarn, leaving a generous tail and work Kitchener st to close.

ARMS

Rnd 1: Using orange and starting in marked st 42 on rnd 91, PU 10 sts, 1 per st to marked st 5. Flip to other end of needle tip, move up 1 rnd and PU same 10 sts, heading back toward first picked-up st. (20 sts). PM in first picked-up st of rnd to indicate beg of rnd.

Rnds 2–48: Knit all sts in stripe patt of 4 rnds orange, 2 rnds black.

Rnds 49–58: With orange, knit all sts.

Rnd 59: K2tog around. (10 sts)

Stuff arm. Cut yarn and using a tapestry needle, pull tail through rem sts to close.

Rep with marked sts 19 and 28 on rnd 91 to make other arm.

FACE

CAPE

TAIL

Rnd 1: Using orange and starting in marked st 57 on rnd 41, PU 8 sts, 1 per st to marked st 64. Slide sts to cable to set up for magic loop method and heading in opposite direction, PU same 8 sts 1 row up. (16 sts). PM in first picked-up st of rnd to indicate beg of rnd.

Rnds 2–90: Knit all sts in stripe patt of 4 rnds orange, 2 rnds black.

Rnds 91–98: With black, knit all sts.

Cut yarn and using a tapestry needle, pull tail through rem sts to close.

EARS

Rnd 1: Using orange and starting in marked st 1 on rnd 138, PU 8 sts, 1 st per rnd toward top of head. Slide sts to cable to set up for magic loop method, move over 1 st toward back of body, and PU same 8 sts, heading in opposite direction. (16 sts). PM in first picked-up st of rnd to indicate beg of rnd.

Rnds 2 and 3: Knit all sts.

Rnd 4: (K1f&b, K6, K1f&b) twice. (20 sts)

Rnds 5–14: Knit all sts.

Rnd 15: K2tog around. (10 sts)

Stuff ear lightly. Cut yarn and use a tapestry needle to pull tail through rem sts to close.

Rep with marked st 32 on rnd 138 to make other ear.

FACE

Using white and your circular needle, CO 4 sts. PM to indicate beg of rnd and beg face using magic loop method.

Rnd 1: K1f&b 4 times. (8 sts)

Rnd 2: K1f&b 8 times. (16 sts)

Rnd 3: Knit all sts.

Rnd 4: (K1f&b, K1) around. (24 sts)

Rnd 5: Knit all sts.

Rnd 6: (K1f&b, K2) around. (32 sts)

Rnd 7: Knit all sts.

Rnd 8: (K1f&b, K3) around. (40 sts)

Rnd 9: Knit all sts.

Rnd 10: (K1f&b, K4) around. (48 sts)

Rnd 11: Knit all sts.

Rnd 12: (K1f&b, K5) around. (56 sts)

Rnd 13: Knit all sts.

Rnd 14: (K1f&b, K6) around. (64 sts)

Rnd 15: Knit all sts.

Rnd 16: (K1f&b, K7) around. (72 sts)

Rnd 17: Knit all sts.

Loosely BO all sts.

> MY SUPER INVISIBILITY POWERS MEAN I JUST HAVE TO TURN MY BACK AND CRIMINALS CAN'T SEE ME!

MASK

Using turquoise and circular needle, CO 64 sts. PM to indicate beg of rnd and beg to work in rnd using magic loop method.

Rnds 1–3: (K2, P2) around.

Rnd 4: K9, BO 6 sts, K1 (2 sts between BO sts), BO 6 sts, knit to end of rnd. (52 sts)

Rnd 5: K9, cable CO 6 sts, K2, cable CO 6 sts, knit to end of rnd. (64 sts)

Rnds 6–17: Knit all sts.

Rnd 18: (K2tog, K6) around. (56 sts)

Rnd 19: Knit all sts.

Rnd 20: (K2tog, K5) around. (48 sts)

Rnd 21: K18, BO 12 sts, K12, BO 12 sts (starting in rnd 21 and ending in next rnd).

Leaving sts that are not attached to working yarn on cable of needle, work sts attached to working yarn back and forth and work 4 more rows in St st. Cut yarn. Do not BO.
Join yarn on opposite live sts on cable. Work 4 rows of St st. Cut working yarn, leaving a long tail to graft 2 sides tog, and work Kitchener st to close.

CAPE BAND, CAPE, AND LIGHTNING BOLT

All are knit flat (back and forth), not in the round.

CAPE BAND

Using turquoise and circular needle, CO 5 sts. DO NOT JOIN.

Knit every row (garter st) for 212 rows, placing removable markers on last st of rows 82 and 130.

CAPE

Row 1 (set up): Using turquoise and starting in marked st on row 82 of cape band, PU 24 sts, 1 st per garter ridge to marked st on row 130.

Row 2: K1f&b in all sts. (48 sts)

Row 3: Knit all sts.

Row 4: K1f&b, knit to last 2 sts, K1f&b, K1. (2-st inc)

Row 5: Knit all sts.

Rows 6–19: Rep rows 4 and 5 another 7 times. (64 sts)

Rows 20–132: Knit all sts.

Loosely BO all sts.

LIGHTNING BOLT

Using aqua or yellow, CO 2 sts. DO NOT JOIN.

Row 1: K1f&b, K1. (3 sts)

Row 2: Knit all sts.

Row 3: K1f&b, K2. (4 sts)

Row 4: Knit all sts.

Row 5: K1f&b, K1f&b, knit to last 2 sts, K2tog. (1 st inc)

Row 6: Knit all sts.

Rows 7–32: Rep rows 5 and 6 another 13 times. (18 sts)

Row 33: BO first 6 sts, K12, cable CO 6 sts. (18 sts)

Row 34: Knit all sts.

Row 35: K1f&b, knit to last 2 sts, K2tog.

Row 36: Knit all sts.

Rows 37–58: Rep rows 35 and 36 another 11 times.

Rows 59 and 60: Rep rows 33 and 34.

Rows 61–88: Rep rows 35 and 36 another 14 times.

Loosely BO all sts.

FINISH TIBERIUS

Pin lightning bolt to center of cape. Using a tapestry needle and matching yarn, sew bolt in place using a running st. Install plastic eyes, or embroider eyes and nose onto face with black scrap yarn. Pin face to center of head. Using a tapestry needle and matching yarn, sew face in place using a running st. Stuff body. Use tapestry needle and matching yarn to whipstitch hole between legs closed. Weave in all rem ends. Throw on Tiberius's mask and cape and go tame some transgressors!

SAMPSON SHEEP

• SUPREME SUPER STYLIST •

Since superheroes tend to have rather complicated, flashy outfits, they all work with stylists. **SAMPSON SHEEP IS THE MOST SUCCESSFUL STYLIST TO THE SUPERS,** and he works with just about every well-known superhero you can think of (although they'll never admit it, since they like to keep this sort of thing private). Sampson is always field testing his creations to make sure they function as intended. The last thing a superhero needs is his super suit not turning invisible when he needs it most!

SAMPLES

COBASI SOCK YARN (below)

* Approx 16" from head to toe
* Colors: Natural 003, Black 002, Kiwi 007
* 9 mm black safety eyes

MERINO WORSTED (at right)

* Approx 22" from head to toe
* Colors: Natural, Licorice, Granny Smith
* 15 mm black safety eyes

MATERIALS

YARN

White: 175–215 yds for sheep, pants, and shoes

Black: 120–195 yds for sheep

Green: 190–215 yds for cape, pants, and shoes

NEEDLES

36" or longer circular needle in a size 2 or 3 sizes smaller than those recommended for your yarn (for magic loop method)

NOTIONS

Basic supplies see ("What to Keep in Your Utility Belt" on page 12)

13 removable st markers (or 12 removable st markers and 1 fixed marker)

2 safety eyes (see "Samples" for sizes)

BODY

Sampson begins at base of body.

Using white and circular needle, use provisional CO to CO 12 sts. DO NOT JOIN.

Rows 1–64: Knit all sts (garter st).

Beg working in the round.

Rnd 1 (set-up rnd): Knit 12 sts, rotate 90° and PU 32 sts, 1 st per garter ridge up edge, place sts from provisional CO on needle tip and K6 of held sts. Slide sts to cable to set up for magic loop method and knit other 6 sts from provisional CO, turn piece 90° and PU 32 sts, 1 st per garter ridge again. (88 sts). K6 of original 12 sts, and adjust sts on needles so that next st is beg of rnd and you are ready to knit using magic loop method. PM in sts 7, 16, 29, and 38 to mark for legs.

Rnds 2 and 3: (K2, P2) around.

Rnds 4 and 5: (P2, K2) around.

Rnds 6–61: Rep rnds 2–5. Place removable markers as you work:

> **Rnd 60:** PM in sts 5, 40, 49, and 84 to mark for arms.

Rnd 62: (K1, K2tog 5 times) 8 times. (48 sts)

Rnds 63 and 64: (P2, K2) around.

Rnds 65 and 66: (K2, P2) around.

Rnds 67–72: Rep rnds 63–66 once more, then just rnds 63 and 64 once.

Beg to stuff body.

Rnd 73: K2, P2, sl 1, K1, P2, (K2, P2) 10 times. Turn. (48 sts)

BACK OF HEAD

Work 32 sts for back of head, working flat (back and forth). Hold rem 16 sts on cable.

Row 1: Sl 1, K1, P2, (K2, P2) to end.

Row 2: Sl 1, K1, P2, (K2, P2) to end.

Row 3: Sl 1, P1, K2, (P2, K2) to end.

Row 4: Sl 1, P1, K2, (P2, K2) to end.

Rows 5–28: Rep rows 1–4 another 6 times.

Rows 29 and 30: Rep rows 1 and 2.

Turn top of head (as for a sock heel turn).

Row 1: Sl 1, K1, P2, (K2, P2) 4 times, P2tog, K1. Turn.

Row 2: Sl 1, P1, ssk, P1. Turn.

Row 3: Sl 1, K2, P2tog, K1. Turn.

Row 4: Sl 1, P1, K2, ssk, K1. Turn.

Row 5: Sl 1, K1, P2, K1, P2tog, P1. Turn.

Row 6: Sl 1, K2, P2, K1, ssk, P1. Turn.

Row 7: Sl 1, P2, K2, P2, P2tog, K1. Turn.

Row 8: Sl 1, K1, P2, K2, P2, ssk, K1. Turn.

Row 9: Sl 1, P1, K2, P2, K2, P1, P2tog, P1. Turn.

Row 10: Sl 1, P2, K2, P2, K2, P1, ssk, P1. Turn.

Row 11: Sl 1, K2, P2, K2, P2, K2, P2tog, K1. Turn.

Row 12: Sl 1, P1, (K2, P2) twice, K2, ssk, K1. Turn.

Row 13: Sl 1, K1, (P2, K2) twice, P2, K1, P2tog, P1. Turn.

Row 14: Sl 1, (K2, P2) 3 times, K1, ssk, P1. Turn.

Row 15: Sl 1, (P2, K2) 3 times, P2, P2tog. Turn.

Row 16: Sl 1, (P2, K2) 3 times, P2, ssk. (16 sts)

FACE

Rnd 1: With black, knit 16 sts at top of head once more. Using same needle tip, PU 18 sts from gusset edge. Slide sts to cable to set up for magic loop method and knit 16 held sts; using same needle tip, PU 18 sts from gusset edge. (68 sts). Knit next 8 sts, next st to be worked is new beg of rnd. Adjust sts on needles to set up working in rnd using magic loop method. PM in sts 7, 14, 56, and 63 to mark for ears. PM to indicate beg of rnd and cont for face.

Rnd 2: Knit all sts.

Rnd 3: (K1, K2tog 8 times) 4 times. (36 sts)

Rnds 4–35: Knit all sts.

Rnd 36: K2tog around. (18 sts)

Rnd 37: Knit all sts.

SHORTS

SHOES

Rnd 38: K2tog around. (9 sts)

Finish stuffing and add safety eyes. Cut yarn and using a tapestry needle, pull tail through rem sts to close.

ARMS

Rnd 1: Using black and starting in marked st 84 on rnd 60, PU 10 sts to marked st 5, 1 per st. Slide sts to cable to set up for magic loop method and heading in opposite direction, PU same 10 sts 1 rnd up. (20 sts). PM in first picked-up st of rnd to indicate beg of rnd.

Rnds 2–60: Knit all sts.

Rnd 61: K2tog around. (10 sts)

Stuff arm. Cut yarn and using a tapestry needle, pull through rem sts to close.

Rep with marked sts 40 and 49 on rnd 60 to make other arm.

EARS

Rnd 1: Using black and starting in marked st 7 on rnd 1 of face, PU 8 sts, 1 per st toward marked st 14. Slide sts to cable to set up for magic loop method and heading in opposite direction, PU same 8 sts 1 st back. (16 sts). PM in first picked-up st of rnd to indicate beg of rnd.

Rnds 2 and 3: Knit all sts.

Rnd 4: (K1f&b, knit to end of needle tip) twice. (18 sts)

Rnd 5: Knit all sts.

Rnd 6: (Knit to last st of needle tip, K1f&b) twice. (20 sts)

Rnd 7: Knit all sts

Rnds 8–11: Rep rnds 4–7. (24 sts)

Rnds 12–25: Knit all sts.

Rnd 26: (K1, ssk, knit to last 3 sts on needle tip, k2tog, K1) twice. (20 sts)

Rnd 27: Knit all sts.

Rnds 28–31: Rep rnds 26 and 27. (12 sts)

Rnd 32: Rep rnd 26. (8 sts)

Stuff ear if desired (samples' ears are unstuffed). Cut yarn and using a tapestry needle, pull tail through rem sts to close.

Rep with marked sts 56 and 63 on rnd 1 of face to make other ear.

LEGS

Rnd 1: Using black and starting in st on base below marked st 7 on rnd 1 of body, PU 10 sts along base to marked st 16. Slide sts to cable to set up for magic loop method and heading in opposite direction, PU same 10 sts 1 rnd up, ending in marked st 7. (20 sts). Be sure beg of rnd is to back of body to ensure correct heel placement, PM.

Rnds 2–50: With black, knit all sts.

Rnds 51–62: With green, knit all sts. Cont in green until noted.

Work heel back and forth in first 10 sts of rnd and holding last 10 sts of rnd on cable of needle.

Row 1: Sl 1 kw, knit to end. Turn.

Row 2: Sl 1 pw, purl to end. Turn.

Rows 3–10: Rep rows 1 and 2.

WORK FOOT

Return to knitting in the round.

Rnd 1: Knit across 10 heel sts once more. Using same needle tip, PU 6 sts from gusset edge. Slide sts to cable to set up for magic loop method, knit 10 held sts. Using same needle tip, PU 6 sts from gusset edge. (32 sts). Beg of rnd is next st to be knitted, PM.

Rnd 2: Knit all sts.

Rnd 3: K10, (K2tog) 3 times, knit to last 6 sts, (ssk) 3 times. (26 sts)

Rnd 4: Knit all sts.

Rnd 5: K10, K2tog, knit to last 2 sts, ssk. (24 sts)

Rnds 6–25: Knit all sts.

Rnds 26–30: With white, knit all sts. Cont in white to end of shoe.

Rnd 31: K2tog around. (12 sts)

Rnd 32: K2tog around. (6 sts)

Stuff shoe. Cut yarn and using a tapestry needle, pull tail through rem sts to close shoe. Using white, crisscross across top of shoe to make shoelaces. Tie ends in a bow.

Rep from rnd 1 of leg with marked sts 29 and 38 on rnd 1 of body to make other leg.

SUPER SHORTS

Using white and circular needle, CO 88 sts. PM to indicate beg of rnd and beg to work in rnd using magic loop method.

Rnds 1–5: With white, (K2, P2) around.

Rnds 6–35: Starting with green, knit all sts in stripe patt of 1 rnd green, 1 rnd white.

Rnd 36: Cont in white, K13, BO 30 sts, K13, BO 30 sts. (28 sts). Cont in white to end of shorts.

Leaving sts that are not attached to working yarn on cable of needle, work sts attached to working yarn back and forth and work 2 rows in St st. Cut yarn. Do not BO.

Join white to opposite live sts that are held on cable. Work 2 rows of St st. Cut yarn, leaving a generous tail. Bring sts tog and work Kitchener st to close shorts.

Finish leg opening.

Rnd 1: Using white, PU 36 sts around leg opening. Work in rnd using magic loop method.

Rnds 2 and 3: (K2, P2) around.

Loosely BO all sts in patt.

Rep rnds 1–3 for other leg opening.

CAPE BAND AND CAPE

Both are knit flat (back and forth), not in the round.

BAND

Using green, CO 4 sts. DO NOT JOIN.

Knit every row (garter st) for 180 rows, placing removable markers on last st of rows 58 and 122.

Loosely BO all sts.

CAPE

Set-up row: Starting in marked st on row 58 of cape band, PU 32 sts, 1 st per garter ridge to marked st on row 122.

Next row (inc): K1f&b 32 times.
(64 sts)

Row 1 (RS): Knit all sts.

Row 2: K2, (P4, K2, P4) across to last 2 sts, K2.

Row 3: K2, (K3, P4, K3) across to last 2 sts, K2.

Row 4: K2, (P2, K6, P2) across to last 2 sts, K2.

Row 5: K2, (K2, P6, K2) across to last 2 sts, K2.

Row 6: Rep row 4.

Row 7: Rep row 3.

Row 8: Rep row 2.

Row 9: Knit all sts.

Row 10: K2, purl to last 2 sts, K2.

Row 11: Knit all sts.

Row 12: K2, purl to last 2 sts, K2.

Row 13: Knit all sts.

Row 14: K2, (K1, P8, K1) across to last 2 sts, K2.

Row 15: Rep row 4.

Row 16: Rep row 3.

Row 17: K2, (P3, K4, P3) across to last 2 sts, K2.

Row 18: Rep row 3.

Row 19: Rep row 4.

Row 20: Rep row 14.

Row 21: Knit all sts.

Row 22: K2, purl to last 2 sts, K2.

Row 23: Knit all sts.

Row 24: K2, purl to last 2 sts, K2.

Rows 25–92: Rep rows 1–24 another 2 times, then work rows 1–20 once more.

Rows 93–96: Knit all sts (garter st).

Loosely BO all sts.

FINISH SAMPSON

Weave in rem ends. Measure a piece of white around Sampson's waist, adding an extra 12" for braiding and tying a bow, and cut 3 pieces that length. Braid 3 pieces into 1 and use a tapestry needle to thread braid through waistband on shorts to create a drawstring. Tie in a bow. Tie on Sampson's cape and go design some super couture.

LANDON LUDWIG

• WONDER KID •

LANDON WAS BORN WITH THE AMAZING POWER TO BRING IMAGINARY FRIENDS TO LIFE. This was quite disconcerting to his family at first, but after a few years (and many therapy sessions), they now think it's great. All Landon has to do is imagine a friend, and that friend pops right into existence. It works with others' imaginary friends as well. This is great for all situations since Landon can always summon the right help, no matter what's going on.

SAMPLES

COBASI SOCK YARN (below)

* Approx 22" from head to toe
* Colors: Raffi 051, Natural 003, Black 002, Turkish Coffee 035, Vavava Voom Red 054, Chocolate Milk 020
* 9 mm black safety eyes

MERINO WORSTED (at right)

* Approx 28" from head to toe
* Colors: Navy, Natural, Licorice, Chocolate/Caramel, Pomegranate
* 1 skein of Shepherd Worsted from Lorna's Laces (100% superwash merino wool; 4 oz; 225 yds) in Chino (skin tone)
* 15 mm black safety eyes

MATERIALS

YARN

Navy: 90–130 yds for pants

White: 40–80 yds for sweater and shoes

Black: 40–80 yds for sweater

Brown: 50–130 yds for hair

Red: 110–170 yds for cape and shoes

Skin Tone: 80–110 yds for face and arms

Waste yarn for holding live sts

Scrap of gold yarn for embroidering jeans

NEEDLES

36" or longer circular needle in a size 2 or 3 sizes smaller than those recommended for your yarn (for magic loop method)

NOTIONS

Basic supplies see ("What to Keep in Your Utility Belt" on page 12)

17 removable st markers (or 16 removable st markers and 1 fixed marker)

2 safety eyes (see "Samples" for sizes)

BODY

Landon begins at base of body.

With navy and circular needle, use provisional CO to CO 8 sts. DO NOT JOIN.

Rows 1–48: Knit all sts (garter st). Set up to work in the round.

Rnd 1: Knit 8 sts again, rotate 90° and PU 24 sts, 1 st per garter ridge up edge, place sts from provisional CO on needle tip and K4 of held sts. Slide sts to cable to set up for magic loop method and knit other 4 sts from provisional CO. Turn piece 90° and PU 24 sts, 1 st per garter ridge again. (64 sts). K4 of original 8 sts, and adjust sts on needles so that next st is beg of rnd and you are ready to knit using magic loop method. Place removable markers in sts 3, 14, 19, and 30 to mark for legs.

Rnds 2–18: With navy, knit all sts.

Rnd 19: With white, (K2tog, K6) around. (56 sts)

Rnds 20 and 21: Cont in white, knit all sts.

Rnds 22–69: With black, knit all sts in stripe patt of 3 rnds black, 3 rnds white. Place removable markers as you work:

> **Rnd 63:** PM in sts 6, 23, 34, and 51 to mark for sleeves.

> **Rnd 65:** PM in sts 4, 25, 32, and 53 to mark for arms.

Rnd 67: PM in sts 6, 23, 34, and 51 to mark for sleeves.

Rnd 70: With black, (K2tog, K2) around. (42 sts). Cont in black until noted.

Rnd 71: Knit all sts.

Rnd 72: [(K2tog) 4 times, K3tog, (K2tog) 5 times] twice. (20 sts)

Beg to stuff body.

Rnds 73–78: With skin tone, knit all sts. Cont with skin tone to top of head.

Rnd 79: [(K1f&b) twice, K2, (K1f&b) twice, K2, (K1f&b) twice] twice. (32 sts)

Rnd 80: Knit all sts.

Rnd 81: (K1f&b, K3) around. (40 sts)

Rnd 82: Knit all sts.

Rnd 83: (K1f&b, K4) around. (48 sts)

Rnd 84: Knit all sts.

Rnd 85: (K1f&b, K5) around. (56 sts)

Rnds 86-110: Knit all sts.

Rnd 111: (K2tog, K5) around. (48 sts)

Rnd 112: Knit all sts.

Rnd 113: (K2tog, K4) around. (40 sts)

Rnd 114: Knit all sts.

Rnd 115: (K2tog, K3) around. (32 sts)

Rnd 116: Knit all sts.

Rnd 117: (K2tog, K2) around. (24 sts)

Cont stuffing body.

Rnd 118: Knit all sts.

Rnd 119: (K2tog, K1) around. (16 sts)

Rnd 120: Knit all sts.

Rnd 121: K2tog around. (8 sts)

Finish stuffing. Cut yarn and use a tapestry needle to pull tail through rem sts, but close head only halfway, do not secure yet, so you can determine safety eye placement once hair is knit.

HAIR

Using brown, CO 4 sts. PM to indicate beg of rnd and beg hair using magic loop method.

Rnd 1: K1f&b 4 times. (8 sts)

Rnd 2 and all even-numbered rnds: Knit all sts.

Rnd 3: K1f&b 8 times. (16 sts)

Rnd 5: (K1f&b, K1) around. (24 sts)

Rnd 7: (K1f&b, K2) around. (32 sts)

Rnd 9: (K1f&b, K3) around. (40 sts)

Rnd 11: (K1f&b, K4) around. (48 sts)

Rnd 13: (K1f&b, K5) around. (56 sts)

Rnd 15: (K1f&b, K6) around. (64 sts)

Rnd 17: (K1f&b, K7) around. (72 sts)

Rnd 18: Knit all sts.

Beg working back and forth to create bangs.

Row 1: Ssk, knit to last 2 sts, K2tog. (70 sts)

Row 2: P2tog, purl to end of row. (69 sts)

FACE

SHOES

Rows 3–8: Rep rows 1 and 2 another 3 times. (60 sts)

Row 9: Knit to last 2 sts, K2tog. (59 sts)

Row 10: P2tog, purl to end of row. (58 sts)

Rows 11–18: Rep rows 9 and 10 another 4 times. (50 sts)

Row 19: Knit all sts.

Row 20: Purl all sts.

Row 21: Knit all sts.

Row 22: Purl all sts.

Row 23: K19, ssk 3 times, K2tog 3 times, knit to end of row. (44 sts)

Row 24: Purl all sts.

Row 25: K16, ssk 3 times, K2tog 3 times, knit to end of row. (38 sts)

Row 26: Purl all sts.

Row 27: K13, ssk 3 times, K2tog 3 times, knit to end of row. (32 sts)

Row 28: Purl all sts.

Row 29: Ssk 3 times, knit to last 6 sts, K2tog 3 times. (26 sts)

Row 30: Purl all sts.

Rows 31 and 32: Rep rows 29 and 30 once more. (20 sts)

Row 33: K2tog across. (10 sts)
Loosely BO all sts.

ARMS

Stitches for arms are picked up from the body and worked partway, then sleeve stitches are picked up from the body and worked around the arm so the arms will be inside the sleeves.

Once the sleeves are done, you'll stuff the arms and work the thumbs.

Rnd 1: Using skin tone and starting in marked st 53 on rnd 65, PU 8 sts, 1 st per rnd to marked st 4. Slide sts to cable to set up for magic loop method and heading in opposite direction, PU same 8 sts 1 rnd up. (16 sts). Be sure beg of rnd is to back of body to ensure correct thumb placement, PM.

Rnds 2–50: Knit all sts.

Rnd 51: (K1f&b, K6, K1f&b) twice. (20 sts)

Rnd 52: (K1f&b, K8, K1f&b) twice. (24 sts)

Rnd 53: K11, K1f&b, K1f&b, K11. (26 sts)

Rnd 54: K12, K1f&b, K1f&b, K12. (28 sts)

Rnd 55: K13, K1f&b, K1f&b, K13. (30 sts)

Rnd 56: K14, K1f&b, K1f&b, K14. (32 sts)

Rnd 57: K12, place next 8 sts on waste yarn. Pulling yarn across gap, knit last 12 sts of rnd. (8 sts on waste yarn for thumb, 24 sts on needles)

Rnds 58–74: Knit all sts.

Rnd 75: (K1, ssk, K6, K2tog, K1) twice. (20 sts)

Cut yarn, leaving a generous tail for Kitchener st. Place sts on waste yarn and cont to knit sleeve. You'll finish hand and thumb once sleeve is finished and arm is stuffed.

Rep with marked st 32 to marked st 25 on rnd 65 to make other arm, again waiting until sleeves are knit to finish.

SLEEVES

Rnd 1: Using white and starting in marked st 51 on rnd 63, PU 12 sts, 1 per st toward marked st 6. Slide sts to cable to set up for magic loop method, move up to marked st 6 on rnd 67 and heading in opposite direction, PU same 12 sts, working toward marked st 51 on rnd 67. You'll be working around arm. (24 sts). As you work sleeve, the gap

from being up several rnds should be unnoticeable. Be sure beg of rnd is to back of arm so jogs from stripes are to back of body, PM.

Rnds 2–24: Cont with white, knit all sts in stripe patt of 3 rnds white, 3 rnds black.

Rnds 25 and 26: With white, knit all sts.

Rnd 27: (K1, P1) around. Loosely BO in patt.

Rep with marked st 34 on rnd 67 and work toward marked st 23 and then from 23 to 34 on rnd 63 to make other sleeve.

Stuff both arms. Place live sts back on needles and work Kitchener st to close arms.

THUMBS

Place 8 sts from waste yarn onto needles. Starting on outside of thumb (away from palm), work in rnd using magic loop method.

Rnd 1: K4, PU 2 from join between thumb and palm, slide sts to cable, PU 2 additional sts from same spot, K4 to end of rnd. (12 sts)

Rnds 2–8: Knit all sts.

Rnd 9: K2tog around. (6 sts)

Stuff hand. Cut yarn and using a tapestry needle, pull through rem sts to close.

Rep on other hand to finish thumb.

LEGS

Rnd 1: Using navy and starting in st on base below marked st 3 on rnd 1, PU 12 sts along base to marked st 14. Slide sts to cable to set up for magic loop method and starting with marked st 14 from rnd 1, PU same 12 sts 1 rnd up toward marked st 3. (24 sts). Be sure beg of rnd is to back of body to ensure correct heel placement, PM.

Rnds 2–80: Knit all sts.

With red, work heel back and forth on first 12 sts of rnd holding last 12 sts of rnd on cable of needle.

Row 1: Sl 1, knit to end. Turn.

Row 2: Sl 1, purl to end. Turn.

Rows 3–6: Rep rows 1 and 2 another 2 times.

Rows 7–12: With white, rep rows 1 and 2 another 3 times.

WORK FOOT

Rnd 1: With red, knit across 12 heel sts again. Using same needle tip, PU 6 sts from gusset edge, slide sts to cable to set up for magic loop method, and knit 12 held sts. Using same needle tip, PU 6 sts from gusset edge. (36 sts). PM in next st to be knitted to indicate beg of rnd.

Rnd 2: K12, (K2tog) twice, K16 to last 4 sts, (ssk) twice. (32 sts). Cont in red until noted.

Rnd 3: Knit all sts.

Rnd 4: K12, (K2tog) twice, K12 to last 4 sts, (ssk) twice. (28 sts)

Rnds 5–30: Knit all sts.

Rnds 31–35: With white, knit all sts.

Cont in white to end of foot.

Rnd 36: K2tog around. (14 sts)

Rnd 37: Knit all sts.

Stuff leg and foot.

Rnd 38: K2tog around. (7 sts)

Finish stuffing. Cut yarn and using a tapestry needle, pull tail through rem sts to close foot.

Using white yarn, crisscross across top of shoe to make shoelaces. Tie ends in a bow.

Rep with marked sts 19 and 30 from rnd 1 of body to make other leg.

CAPE AND CAPE BAND

Both are knit flat (back and forth), not in the round.

CAPE

Using red, CO 20 sts. DO NOT JOIN.

Rows 1–4: Knit all sts (garter st).

Rows 5–8: Work in St st.

Row 9: K1, K1f&b, knit to last 2 sts, K1f&b, K1. (22 sts)

Rows 10–12: Knit all sts.

I'M JUSTICE'S NONIMAGINARY FRIEND!

Rows 13–132: Rep rows 5–12 another 15 times. (16 garter stripes and 52 sts)

Loosely BO all sts.

BAND

Using red, PU 6 sts along top edge of cape. DO NOT JOIN.

Rows 1–48: Knit all sts.

Slide empty needle tip through 6 sts on opposite top side of cape, and working on "inside" of cape, use 3-needle BO to BO and join cape band to opposite side of cape.

FINISH LANDON

Place hair on head and determine safety eye placement. Attach safety eyes and then close head, weaving in ends. Place hair back on head and with tapestry needle and matching yarn, use a running st to sew hair to head. Embroider mouth using black. Using gold and photos as a guide, embroider front and back pockets and fly onto jeans. Weave in all rem ends. Block cape as desired. Slip cape over Landon's head and find your own real-life Wonder Kid for a super adventure!

MAKE A SUPER GIRL!

Wanna make a super girl? Use long pieces of hair-colored yarn to make pigtails. Or, skip the knit hair entirely and do an online search for "Knitted Doll Hair Tutorials" for other fun ways to make doll hair.

ALA-SHAZAM!

WHERE TO GET THE GOODS

Contact the following yarn companies to find shops in your area that carry the yarns featured in this book.

ANOTHER CRAFTY GIRL

www.anothercraftygirl.com
Merino Worsted

HIKOO Distributed by Skacel

http://www.skacelknitting.com
CoBaSi

LION BRAND YARN

www.lionbrand.com
Romance

LORNA'S LACES

www.lornaslaces.net
Shepherd Worsted

All buttons were purchased at Hobby Lobby.

ABBREVIATIONS

( ) Work instructions within parentheses as many times as directed

Approx Approximately

beg begin(ning)

BO bind off

cable CO cable cast on: with stitches on left needle, insert needle between first 2 stitches. Wrap yarn around the right needle and pull through to make a stitch. Place new stitch on left needle—1 stitch added to left needle. Repeat as needed.

CO cast on

cont continue(ing)(s)

dec(s) decrease(ing)(s)

dpn(s) double-pointed needle(s)

est established

garter st garter stitch: in the round—knit 1 round, purl 1 round; back and forth—knit every row

I-cord using 2 double-pointed needles, cast on specified number of stitches; usually 3 or 4. *Knit the stitches, do NOT turn, slide stitches to other end of needle. Pulling yarn firmly across the back, repeat from * until cord is required length.

inc(s) increase(ing)(s)

join begin to knit in the round

K knit

K1f&b knit into front and back of same stitch—1 stitch increased

K2tog knit 2 stitches together—1 stitch decreased

knitted CO knitted cast on: with stitches on left needle, knit the first stitch but leave stitch on the left needle, rotate right needle clockwise and insert tip of left needle into the stitch from left to right and remove from right needle—1 stitch added to left needle. Repeat as needed.

kw knitwise

LH left hand

mm millimeter(s)

oz ounce(s)

P purl

P1f&b purl into front and back of same stitch—1 stitch increased

P2tog purl 2 stitches together—1 stitch decreased

patt(s) pattern(s)

pick up slide needle through stitch placing loop on needle; repeat for required number of stitches

PM place marker

PU pick up and knit: insert right needle into stitch and pull working yarn through stitch and onto right needle—1 stitch picked up. Repeat as needed.

pw purlwise

rem remain(ing)(s)

rep(s) repeat(s)

RH right hand

rnd(s) round(s)

RS right side

sl slip

sl 1 slip 1 stitch as if to purl unless otherwise indicated

SM slip marker

ssk slip 2 stitches knitwise, 1 at a time, to right needle, then insert left needle from left to right into front loops and knit 2 stitches together—1 stitch decreased

st(s) stitch(es)

St st(s) stockinette stitch(es): in the round—knit every round; back and forth—knit on right side, purl on wrong side

tbl through back loop(s)

tog together

Turkish CO Turkish cast on: make a slipknot and place on one of two double-pointed needles. Hold needles parallel and wrap yarn around both needles until there are the number of specified loops (per your pattern) on each needle. Hold the tail down with your left thumb, and use a third needle to knit the loops of the top needle without letting the loops on the bottom needle slide off. Turn, with another needle, knit the loops off the bottom needle through the back of the loop to keep them from being twisted. Knit the stitches on each needle one more time. Continue with instructions for your project.

WS wrong side

yd(s) yard(s)

USEFUL INFORMATION

STANDARD YARN-WEIGHT SYSTEM						
Yarn-Weight Symbol and Category Name	**1** Super Fine	**2** Fine	**3** Light	**4** Medium	**5** Bulky	**6** Super Bulky
Types of Yarn in Category	Sock, Fingering, Baby	Sport, Baby	DK, Light Worsted	Worsted, Afghan, Aran	Chunky, Craft, Rug	Bulky, Roving
Knit Gauge Range* in Stockinette Stitch to 4"	27 to 32 sts	23 to 26 sts	21 to 24 sts	16 to 20 sts	12 to 15 sts	6 to 11 sts
Recommended Needle in Metric Size Range	2.25 to 3.25 mm	3.25 to 3.75 mm	3.75 to 4.5 mm	4.5 to 5.5 mm	5.5 to 8 mm	8 mm and larger
Recommended Needle in US Size Range	1 to 3	3 to 5	5 to 7	7 to 9	9 to 11	11 and larger

These are guidelines only. The above reflect the most commonly used gauges and needles for specific yarn categories.

METRIC CONVERSIONS

Yards x .91 = meters
Meters x 1.09 = yards
Ounces x 28.35 = grams
Grams x .035 = ounces